The Constitution of the
State of Virginia:
A Quick Reference Guide

Bootblack Budget Books
Copyright 2018 ©
ISBN-13: 978-1724776051
ISBN-10: 1724776053

Contents:

Preamble – Page 16

Article I: Bill of Rights – Page 17

Section 1: Equality and Rights of Men

Section 2: People the Source of Power

Section 3: Government Instituted for Common Benefit

Section 4: No Exclusive Emoluments or Privileges; Offices not to be Hereditary

Section 5: Separation of Legislative, Executive, and Judicial Departments; Periodical Elections

Section 6: Free Elections; Consent of Governed

Section 7: Laws Should not be Suspended

Section 8: Criminal Prosecutions

Section 8-A: Rights of Victims of Crime

Section 9: Prohibition of Excessive Bail and Fines, Cruel and Unusual Punishment, Suspension of Habeas Corpus, Bills of Attainder, and Ex Post Facto Laws

Section 10: General Warrants of Search or Seizure Prohibited

Section 11: Due Process of Law; Obligation of Contracts; Taking or Damaging of Private Property; Prohibited Discrimination; Jury Trial in Civil Cases

Section 12: Freedom of Speech and of the Press; Right Peaceably to Assemble, and to Petition

Section 13: Militia; Standing Armies; Military Subordinate to Civil Power

Section 14: Government Should be Uniform

Section 15: Qualities Necessary to Preservation of Free Government

Section 15-A: Marriage

Section 16: Free Exercise of Religion; No Establishment of Religion

Section 17: Construction of the Bill Of Rights

Article II: Franchise and Officers – Page 25

Section 1: Qualifications of Voters

Section 2: Registration of Voters

Section 3: Method of Voting

Section 4: Powers and Duties of General Assembly

Section 5: Qualifications to Hold Elective Office

Section 6: Apportionment

Section 7: Oath or Affirmation

Section 8: Electoral Boards; Registrars and Officers Of Election

Section 9: Privileges of Voters During Election

Article III: Division of Powers – Page 31

Section 1: Departments to be Distinct

Article IV: Legislature – Page 32

Section 1: Legislative Power

Section 2: Senate

Section 3: House of Delegates

Section 4: Qualifications of Senators and Delegates

Section 5: Compensation; Election to Civil Office of Profit

Section 6: Legislative Sessions

Section 7: Organization of General Assembly

Section 8: Quorum

Section 9: Immunity of Legislators

Section 10: Journal of Proceedings

Section 11: Enactment of Laws

Section 12: Form of Laws

Section 13: Effective Date of Laws

Section 14: Powers of General Assembly; Limitations

Section 15: General Laws

Section 16: Appropriations to Religious or Charitable Bodies

Section 17: Impeachment

Section 18: Auditor of Public Accounts

Article V: Executive – Page 43

Section 1: Executive Power; Governor's Term of Office

Section 2: Election of Governor

Section 3: Qualifications of Governor

Section 4: Place of Residence and Compensation of Governor

Section 5: Legislative Responsibilities of Governor

Section 6: Presentation of Bills; Powers of Governor; Vetoes and Amendments

Section 7: Executive and Administrative Powers

Section 8: Information from Administrative Officers

Section 9: Administrative Organization

Section 10: Appointment and Removal of Administrative Officers

Section 11: Effect of Refusal of General Assembly to Confirm an Appointment by the Governor

Section 12: Executive Clemency

Section 13: Lieutenant Governor; Election and Qualifications

Section 14: Duties and Compensation of Lieutenant Governor

Section 15: Attorney General

Section 16: Succession to the Office of Governor

Section 17: Commissions and Grants

Article VI: Judiciary – Page 53

Section 1: Judicial Power; Jurisdiction

Section 2: Supreme Court

Section 3: Selection of Chief Justice

Section 4: Administration of the Judicial System

Section 5: Rules of Practice and Procedure

Section 6: Opinions and Judgments of the Supreme Court

Section 7: Selection and Qualification of Judges

Section 8: Additional Judicial Personnel

Section 9: Commission; Compensation; Retirement

Section 10: Disabled and Unfit Judges

Section 11: Incompatible Activities

Section 12: Limitation; Judicial Appointment

Article VII: Local Government – Page 59

Section 1: Definitions

Section 2: Organization and Government

Section 3: Powers

Section 4: County and City Officers

Section 5: County, City, and Town Governing Bodies

Section 6: Multiple Offices

Section 7: Procedures

Section 8: Consent to Use Public Property

Section 9: Sale of Property and Granting of Franchises by Cities and Towns

Section 10: Debt

Article VIII: Education – Page 67

Section 1: Public Schools of High Quality to be Maintained

Section 2: Standards of Quality; State and Local Support of Public Schools

Section 3: Compulsory Education; Free Textbooks

Section 4: Board of Education

Section 5: Powers and Duties of the Board of Education

Section 6: Superintendent of Public Instruction

Section 7: School Boards

Section 8: The Literary Fund

Section 9: Other Educational Institutions

Section 10: State Appropriations Prohibited to Schools or Institutions of Learning not Owned or Exclusively Controlled by the State or Some Subdivision Thereof; Exceptions to Rule

Section 11: Aid to Nonpublic Higher Education

Article IX: Corporations – Page 72

Section 1: State Corporation Commission

Section 2: Powers and Duties of the Commission

Section 3: Procedures of the Commission

Section 4: Appeals From Actions of the Commission

Section 5: Foreign Corporations

Section 6: Corporations Subject to General Laws

Section 7: Exclusions From Term "Corporation" or "Company"

Article X: Taxation and Finance – Page 76

Section 1: Taxable Property; Uniformity; Classification and Segregation

Section 2: Assessments

Section 3: Taxes or Assessments Upon Abutting Property Owners

Section 4: Property Segregated for Local Taxation; Exceptions

Section 5: Franchise Taxes; Taxation of Corporate Stock

Section 6: Exempt Property

Section 6-A: Property Tax Exemption for Certain Veterans and Surviving Spouses of Soldiers Killed in Action

Section 6-B: Property Tax Exemptions for Spouses of Certain Emergency Services Providers

Section 7: Collection and Disposition of State Revenues

Section 7-A: Lottery Proceeds Fund; Distribution of Lottery Revenues

Section 8: Limit of Tax or Revenue; Revenue Stabilization Fund

Section 9: State Debt

Section 10: Lending of Credit, Stock Subscriptions, and Works of Internal Improvement

Section 11: Governmental Employees Retirement System

Article XI: Conservation – Page 91

Section 1: Natural Resources and Historical Sites of the Commonwealth

Section 2: Conservation and Development of Natural Resources and Historical Sites

Section 3: Natural Oyster Beds

Section 4: Right of the People to Hunt, Fish, and Harvest Game

Article XII: Future Changes – Page 93

Section 1: Amendments

Section 2: Constitutional Convention

Schedule – Page 95

Section 1: Effective Date of Revised Constitution

Section 2: Officers and Elections

Section 3: Laws, Proceedings, and Obligations Unaffected

Section 4: Qualifications of Judges

Section 5: First Session of General Assembly Following Adoption of Revised Constitution

Preamble:

A DECLARATION OF RIGHTS made by the good people of Virginia in the exercise of their sovereign powers, which rights do pertain to them and their posterity, as the basis and foundation of government.

ARTICLE I: BILL OF RIGHTS

Section 1. Equality and Rights of Men

That all men are by nature equally free and independent and have certain inherent rights, of which, when they enter into a state of society, they cannot, by any compact, deprive or divest their posterity; namely, the enjoyment of life and liberty, with the means of acquiring and possessing property, and pursuing and obtaining happiness and safety.

Section 2. People the Source of Power

That all power is vested in, and consequently derived from, the people, that magistrates are their trustees and servants, and at all times amenable to them.

Section 3. Government Instituted for Common Benefit

That government is, or ought to be, instituted for the common benefit, protection, and security of the people, nation, or community; of all the various modes and forms of government, that is best which is capable of producing the greatest degree of happiness and safety, and is most effectually secured against the danger of maladministration; and, whenever any government shall be found inadequate or contrary to these purposes, a majority of the community hath an indubitable, inalienable, and indefeasible right to reform, alter, or abolish it, in such manner as shall be judged most conducive to the public weal.

Section 4. No Exclusive Emoluments or Privileges; Offices not To be Hereditary

That no man, or set of men, is entitled to exclusive or separate emoluments or privileges from the community, but in consideration of public services; which not being descendible, neither ought the offices of magistrate, legislator, or judge to be hereditary.

Section 5. Separation of Legislative, Executive, and Judicial Departments; Periodical Elections.

That the legislative, executive, and judicial departments of the Commonwealth should be separate and distinct; and that the members thereof may be restrained from oppression, by feeling and participating the burthens of the people, they should, at fixed periods, be reduced to a private station, return into that body from which they were originally taken, and the vacancies be supplied by regular elections, in which all or any part of the former members shall be again eligible, or ineligible, as the laws may direct.

Section 6. Free Elections; Consent of Governed

That all elections ought to be free; and that all men, having sufficient evidence of permanent common interest with, and attachment to, the community, have the right of suffrage, and cannot be taxed, or deprived of, or damaged in, their property for public uses, without their own consent, or that of their representatives duly elected, or bound by any law to which they have not, in like manner, assented for the public good.

Section 7. Laws Should not be Suspended

That all power of suspending laws, or the execution of laws, by any authority, without consent of the representatives of the people, is injurious to their rights, and ought not to be exercised.

Section 8. Criminal Prosecutions

That in criminal prosecutions a man hath a right to demand the cause and nature of his accusation, to be confronted with the accusers and witnesses, and to call for evidence in his favor, and he shall enjoy the right to a speedy and public trial, by an impartial jury of his vicinage, without whose unanimous consent he cannot be found guilty. He shall not be deprived of life or liberty, except by the law of the land or the judgment of his peers, nor be compelled in any criminal proceeding to give evidence against himself, nor be put twice in jeopardy for the same offense.

Laws may be enacted providing for the trial of offenses not felonious by a court not of record without a jury, preserving the right of the accused to an appeal to and a trial by jury in some court of record having original criminal jurisdiction. Laws may also provide for juries consisting of less than twelve, but not less than five, for the trial of offenses not felonious, and may classify such cases, and prescribe the number of jurors for each class. In criminal cases, the accused may plead guilty. If the accused plead not guilty, he may, with his consent and the concurrence of the Commonwealth's Attorney and of the court entered of record, be tried by a smaller number of jurors, or waive a jury. In case of such waiver or plea of guilty, the court shall try the case. The provisions of this section shall be self-executing.

Section 8-A. Rights of Victims of Crime

That in criminal prosecutions, the victim shall be accorded fairness, dignity and respect by the officers, employees and agents of the Commonwealth and its political subdivisions and officers of the courts and, as the General Assembly may define and provide by law, may be accorded rights to reasonable and appropriate notice, information, restitution, protection, and access to a meaningful role in the criminal justice process. These rights may include, but not be limited to, the following:

1. The right to protection from further harm or reprisal through the imposition of appropriate bail and conditions of release;

2. The right to be treated with respect, dignity and fairness at all stages of the criminal justice system;

3. The right to address the circuit court at the time sentence is imposed;

4. The right to receive timely notification of judicial proceedings;

5. The right to restitution;

6. The right to be advised of release from custody or escape of the offender, whether before or after disposition; and

7. The right to confer with the prosecution

This section does not confer upon any person a right to appeal or modify any decision in a criminal proceeding, does not abridge any other right guaranteed by the Constitution of the United States or this Constitution, and does not create any cause of action for compensation or damages against the Commonwealth or any of its political subdivisions, any officer, employee or agent of the Commonwealth or any of its political subdivisions, or any officer of the court.

Section 9. Prohibition of Excessive Bail and Fines, Cruel and Unusual Punishment, Suspension of Habeas Corpus, Bills of Attainder, and Ex Post Facto Laws

That excessive bail ought not to be required, nor excessive fines imposed, nor cruel and unusual punishments inflicted; that the privilege of the writ of habeas corpus shall not be suspended unless when, in cases of invasion or rebellion, the public safety may require; and that the General Assembly shall not pass any bill of attainder, or any ex post facto law.

Section 10. General Warrants of Search or Seizure Prohibited

That general warrants, whereby an officer or messenger may be commanded to search suspected places without evidence of a fact committed, or to seize any person or persons not named, or whose offense is not particularly described and supported by evidence, are grievous and oppressive, and ought not to be granted.

Section 11. Due Process of Law; Obligation of Contracts; Taking or Damaging of Private Property; Prohibited Discrimination; Jury Trial in Civil Cases

That no person shall be deprived of his life, liberty, or property without due process of law; that the General Assembly shall not pass any law impairing the obligation of contracts; and that the right to be free from any governmental discrimination upon the basis of religious conviction, race, color, sex, or national origin shall not be abridged, except that the mere separation of the sexes shall not be considered discrimination.

That in controversies respecting property, and in suits between man and man, trial by jury is preferable to any other, and ought to be held sacred. The General Assembly may limit the number of jurors for civil cases in courts of record to not less than five. That the General Assembly shall pass no law whereby private property, the right to which is fundamental, shall be damaged or taken except for public use. No private property shall be damaged or taken for public use without just compensation to the owner thereof. No more private property may be taken than necessary to achieve the stated public use. Just compensation shall be no less than the value of the property taken, lost profits and lost access, and damages to the residue caused by the taking. The terms "lost profits" and "lost access" are to be defined by the General Assembly. A public service company, public service corporation, or railroad exercises the power of eminent domain for public use when such exercise is for the authorized provision of utility, common carrier, or railroad services. In all other cases, a taking or damaging of private property is not for public use if the primary use is for private gain, private benefit, private enterprise, increasing jobs, increasing tax revenue, or economic development, except for the elimination of a public nuisance existing on the property. The condemnor bears the burden of proving that the use is public, without a presumption that it is.

Section 12. Freedom of Speech and of the Press; Right Peaceably to Assemble, and to Petition

That the freedoms of speech and of the press are among the great bulwarks of liberty, and can never be restrained except by despotic governments; that any citizen may freely speak, write, and publish his sentiments on all subjects, being responsible for the abuse of that right; that the General Assembly shall not pass any law abridging the freedom of speech or of the press, nor the right of the people peaceably to assemble, and to petition the government for the redress of grievances.

Section 13. Militia; Standing Armies; Military Subordinate to Civil Power

That a well regulated militia, composed of the body of the people, trained to arms, is the proper, natural, and safe defense of a free state, therefore, the right of the people to keep and bear arms shall not be infringed; that standing armies, in time of peace, should be avoided as dangerous to liberty; and that in all cases the military should be under strict subordination to, and governed by, the civil power.

Section 14. Government Should be Uniform

That the people have a right to uniform government; and, therefore, that no government separate from, or independent of, the government of Virginia, ought to be erected or established within the limits thereof.

Section 15. Qualities Necessary to Preservation of Free Government

That no free government, nor the blessings of liberty, can be preserved to any people, but by a firm adherence to justice, moderation, temperance, frugality, and virtue; by frequent recurrence to fundamental principles; and by the recognition by all citizens that they have duties as well as rights, and that such rights cannot be enjoyed save in a society where law is respected and due process is observed.

That free government rests, as does all progress, upon the broadest possible diffusion of knowledge, and that the Commonwealth should avail itself of those talents which nature has sown so liberally among its people by assuring the opportunity for their fullest development by an effective system of education throughout the Commonwealth.

Section 15-A. Marriage

That only a union between one man and one woman may be a marriage valid in or recognized by this Commonwealth and its political subdivisions. This Commonwealth and its political subdivisions shall not create or recognize a legal status for relationships of unmarried individuals that intends to approximate the design, qualities, significance, or effects of marriage. Nor shall this Commonwealth or its political subdivisions create or recognize another union, partnership, or other legal status to which is assigned the rights, benefits, obligations, qualities, or effects of marriage.

Section 16. Free Exercise of Religion; No Establishment of Religion

That religion or the duty which we owe to our Creator, and the manner of discharging it, can be directed only by reason and conviction, not by force or violence; and, therefore, all men are equally entitled to the free exercise of religion, according to the dictates of conscience; and that it is the mutual duty of all to practice Christian forbearance, love, and charity towards each other. No man shall be compelled to frequent or support any religious worship, place, or ministry whatsoever, nor shall be enforced, restrained, molested, or burthened in his body or goods, nor shall otherwise suffer on account of his religious opinions or belief; but all men shall be free to profess and by argument to maintain their opinions in matters of religion, and the same shall in nowise diminish, enlarge, or affect their civil capacities. And the General Assembly shall not prescribe any religious test whatever, or confer any peculiar privileges or advantages on any sect or denomination, or pass any law requiring or authorizing any religious society, or the people of any district within this Commonwealth, to levy on themselves or others, any tax for the erection or repair of any house of public worship, or for the support of any church or ministry; but it shall be left free to every person to select his religious instructor, and to make for his support such private contract as he shall please.

Section 17. Construction of the Bill of Rights

The rights enumerated in this Bill of Rights shall not be construed to limit other rights of the people not therein expressed.

ARTICLE II: FRANCHISE AND OFFICERS

Section 1. Qualifications of Voters

In elections by the people, the qualifications of voters shall be as follows: Each voter shall be a citizen of the United States, shall be eighteen years of age, shall fulfill the residence requirements set forth in this section, and shall be registered to vote pursuant to this article. No person who has been convicted of a felony shall be qualified to vote unless his civil rights have been restored by the Governor or other appropriate authority. As prescribed by law, no person adjudicated to be mentally incompetent shall be qualified to vote until his competency has been reestablished.

The residence requirements shall be that each voter shall be a resident of the Commonwealth and of the precinct where he votes. Residence, for all purposes of qualification to vote, requires both domicile and a place of abode. The General Assembly may provide for persons who are employed overseas, and their spouses and dependents residing with them, and who are qualified to vote except for relinquishing their place of abode in the Commonwealth while overseas, to vote in the Commonwealth subject to conditions and time limits defined by law. The General Assembly may provide for persons who are qualified to vote except for having moved their residence from one precinct to another within the Commonwealth to continue to vote in a former precinct subject to conditions and time limits defined by law. The General Assembly may also provide, in elections for President and Vice-President of the United States, alternatives to registration for new residents of the Commonwealth.

Any person who will be qualified with respect to age to vote at the next general election shall be permitted to register in advance and also to vote in any intervening primary or special election.

Section 2. Registration of Voters

The General Assembly shall provide by law for the registration of all persons otherwise qualified to vote who have met the residence requirements contained in this article, and shall ensure that the opportunity to register is made available. Registrations accomplished prior to the effective date of this section shall be effective hereunder. The registration records shall not be closed to new or transferred registrations more than thirty days before the election in which they are to be used.

Applications to register shall require the applicant to provide the following information on a standard form: full name; date of birth; residence address; social security number, if any; whether the applicant is presently a United States citizen; and such additional information as may be required by law. All applications to register shall be completed by or at the direction of the applicant and signed by the applicant, unless physically disabled. No fee shall be charged to the applicant incident to an application to register.

Nothing in this article shall preclude the General Assembly from requiring as a prerequisite to registration to vote the ability of the applicant to read and complete in his own handwriting the application to register.

Section 3. Method of Voting

In elections by the people, the following safeguards shall be maintained: Voting shall be by ballot or by machines for receiving, recording, and counting votes cast. No ballot or list of candidates upon any voting machine shall bear any distinguishing mark or symbol, other than words identifying political party affiliation; and their form, including the offices to be filled and the listing of candidates or nominees, shall be as uniform as is practicable throughout the Commonwealth or smaller governmental unit in which the election is held.

In elections other than primary elections, provision shall be made whereby votes may be cast for persons other than the listed candidates or nominees. Secrecy in casting votes shall be maintained, except as provision may be made for assistance to handicapped voters, but the ballot box or voting machine shall be kept in public view and shall not be opened, nor the ballots canvassed nor the votes counted, in secret. Votes may be cast in person or by absentee ballot as provided by law.

Section 4. Powers and Duties of General Assembly

The General Assembly shall establish a uniform system for permanent registration of voters pursuant to this Constitution, including provisions for appeal by any person denied registration, correction of illegal or fraudulent registrations, penalties for illegal, fraudulent, or false registrations, proper transfer of all registered voters, and cancellation of registrations in other jurisdictions of persons who apply to register to vote in the Commonwealth. The General Assembly shall provide for maintenance of accurate and current registration records and may provide for the cancellation of registrations for such purpose.

The General Assembly shall provide for the nomination of candidates, shall regulate the time, place, manner, conduct, and administration of primary, general, and special elections, and shall have power to make any other law regulating elections not inconsistent with this Constitution.

Section 5. Qualifications to Hold Elective Office

The only qualification to hold any office of the Commonwealth or of its governmental units, elective by the people, shall be that a person must have been a resident of the Commonwealth for one year next preceding his election and be qualified to vote for that office, except as otherwise provided in this Constitution, and except that:

(a) the General Assembly may impose more restrictive geographical residence requirements for election of its members, and may permit other governing bodies in the Commonwealth to impose more restrictive geographical residence requirements for election to such governing bodies, but no such requirements shall impair equal representation of the persons entitled to vote;

(b) the General Assembly may provide that residence in a local governmental unit is not required for election to designated elective offices in local governments, other than membership in the local governing body; and

(c) nothing in this Constitution shall limit the power of the General Assembly to prevent conflict of interests, dual officeholding, or other incompatible activities by elective or appointive officials of the Commonwealth or of any political subdivision.

Section 6. Apportionment

Members of the House of Representatives of the United States and members of the Senate and of the House of Delegates of the General Assembly shall be elected from electoral districts established by the General Assembly. Every electoral district shall be composed of contiguous and compact territory and shall be so constituted as to give, as nearly as is practicable, representation in proportion to the population of the district. The General Assembly shall reapportion the Commonwealth into electoral districts in accordance with this section in the year 2011 and every ten years thereafter.

Any such decennial reapportionment law shall take effect immediately and not be subject to the limitations contained in Article IV, Section 13, of this Constitution.

The districts delineated in the decennial reapportionment law shall be implemented for the November general election for the United States House of Representatives, Senate, or House of

Delegates, respectively, that is held immediately prior to the expiration of the term being served in the year that the reapportionment law is required to be enacted. A member in office at the time that a decennial redistricting law is enacted shall complete his term of office and shall continue to represent the district from which he was elected for the duration of such term of office so long as he does not move his residence from the district from which he was elected. Any vacancy occurring during such term shall be filled from the same district that elected the member whose vacancy is being filled.

Section 7. Oath or Affirmation.

All officers elected or appointed under or pursuant to this Constitution shall, before they enter on the performance of their public duties, severally take and subscribe the following oath or affirmation:

"I do solemnly swear (or affirm) that I will support the Constitution of the United States, and the Constitution of the Commonwealth of Virginia, and that I will faithfully and impartially discharge all the duties incumbent upon me as ...., according to the best of my ability (so help me God)."

Section 8. Electoral Boards; Registrars and Officers of Election

There shall be in each county and city an electoral board composed of three members, selected as provided by law. In the appointment of the electoral boards, representation, as far as practicable, shall be given to each of the two political parties which, at the general election next preceding their appointment, cast the highest and the next highest number of votes. The present members of such boards shall continue in office until the expiration of their respective terms; thereafter their successors shall be appointed for the term of three years. Any vacancy occurring in any board shall be filled by the same authority for the unexpired term.

Each electoral board shall appoint the officers of election and general registrar for its county or city. In appointing such officers of election, representation, as far as practicable, shall be given to each of the two political parties which, at the general election next preceding their appointment, cast the highest and next highest number of votes.

No person, nor the deputy of any person, who is employed by or holds any office or post of profit or emolument, or who holds any elective office of profit or trust, under the governments of the United States, the Commonwealth, or any county, city, or town, shall be appointed a member of the electoral board or general registrar. No person, nor the deputy or the employee of any person, who holds any elective office of profit or trust under the government of the United States, the Commonwealth, or any county, city, or town of the Commonwealth shall be appointed an assistant registrar or officer of election.

Section 9. Privileges of Voters During Election

No voter, during the time of holding any election at which he is entitled to vote, shall be compelled to perform military service, except in time of war or public danger, nor to attend any court as suitor, juror, or witness; nor shall any such voter be subject to arrest under any civil process during his attendance at election or in going to or returning therefrom.

ARTICLE III: DIVISION OF POWERS

Section 1. Departments to be Distinct

The legislative, executive, and judicial departments shall be separate and distinct, so that none exercise the powers properly belonging to the others, nor any person exercise the power of more than one of them at the same time; provided, however, administrative agencies may be created by the General Assembly with such authority and duties as the General Assembly may prescribe. Provisions may be made for judicial review of any finding, order, or judgment of such administrative agencies.

ARTICLE IV: LEGISLATURE

Section 1. Legislative Power

The legislative power of the Commonwealth shall be vested in a General Assembly, which shall consist of a Senate and House of Delegates.

Section 2. Senate

The Senate shall consist of not more than forty and not less than thirty-three members, who shall be elected quadrennially by the voters of the several senatorial districts on the Tuesday succeeding the first Monday in November.

Section 3. House of Delegates

The House of Delegates shall consist of not more than one hundred and not less than ninety members, who shall be elected biennially by the voters of the several house districts on the Tuesday succeeding the first Monday in November.

Section 4. Qualifications of Senators and Delegates

Any person may be elected to the Senate who, at the time of the election, is twenty-one years of age, is a resident of the senatorial district which he is seeking to represent, and is qualified to vote for members of the General Assembly. Any person may be elected to the House of Delegates who, at the time of the election, is twenty-one years of age, is a resident of the house district which he is seeking to represent, and is qualified to vote for members of the General Assembly. A senator or delegate who moves his residence from the district for which he is elected shall thereby vacate his office.

No person holding a salaried office under the government of the Commonwealth, and no judge of any court, attorney for the Commonwealth, sheriff, treasurer, assessor of taxes, commissioner of the revenue, collector of taxes, or clerk of any court shall be a member of either house of the General Assembly during his continuance in office; and his qualification as a member shall vacate any such office held by him. No person holding any office or post of profit or emolument under the United States government, or who is in the employment of such government, shall be eligible to either house.

Section 5. Compensation; Election to Civil Office of Profit

The members of the General Assembly shall receive such salary and allowances as may be prescribed by law, but no increase in salary shall take effect for a given member until after the end of the term for which he was elected. No member during the term for which he shall have been elected shall be elected by the General Assembly to any civil office of profit in the Commonwealth.

Section 6. Legislative Sessions

The General Assembly shall meet once each year on the second Wednesday in January. Except as herein provided for reconvened sessions, no regular session of the General Assembly convened in an even-numbered year shall continue longer than sixty days; no regular session of the General Assembly convened in an odd-numbered year shall continue longer than thirty days; but with the concurrence of two-thirds of the members elected to each house, any regular session may be extended for a period not exceeding thirty days. Neither house shall, without the consent of the other, adjourn to another place, nor for more than three days.

The Governor may convene a special session of the General Assembly when, in his opinion, the interest of the Commonwealth may require and shall convene a special session upon the application of two-thirds of the members elected to each house.

The General Assembly shall reconvene on the sixth Wednesday after adjournment of each regular or special session for the purpose of considering bills which may have been returned by the Governor with recommendations for their amendment and bills and items of appropriation bills which may have been returned by the Governor with his objections. No other business shall be considered at a reconvened session. Such reconvened session shall not continue longer than three days unless the session be extended, for a period not exceeding seven additional days, upon the vote of the majority of the members elected to each house. The General Assembly may provide, by a joint resolution approved during a regular or special session by the vote of the majority of the members elected to each house, that it shall reconvene on a date after the sixth Wednesday after adjournment of the regular or special session but no later than the seventh Wednesday after adjournment.

Section 7. Organization of General Assembly

The House of Delegates shall choose its own Speaker; and, in the absence of the Lieutenant Governor, or when he shall exercise the office of Governor, the Senate shall choose from its own body a president pro tempore. Each house shall select its officers and settle its rules of procedure. The houses may jointly provide for legislative continuity between sessions occurring during the term for which members of the House of Delegates are elected. Each house may direct writs of election for supplying vacancies which may occur during a session of the General Assembly. If vacancies exist while the General Assembly is not in session, such writs may be issued by the Governor under such regulations as may be prescribed by law. Each house shall judge of the election, qualification, and returns of its members, may punish them for disorderly behavior, and, with the concurrence of two-thirds of its elected membership, may expel a member.

Section 8. Quorum

A majority of the members elected to each house shall constitute a quorum to do business, but a smaller number may adjourn from day to day and shall have power to compel the attendance of members in such manner and under such penalty as each house may prescribe. A smaller number, not less than two-fifths of the elected membership of each house, may meet and may, notwithstanding any other provision of this Constitution, enact legislation if the Governor by proclamation declares that a quorum of the General Assembly cannot be convened because of enemy attack upon the soil of Virginia. Such legislation shall remain effective only until thirty days after a quorum of the General Assembly can be convened.

Section 9. Immunity of Legislators

Members of the General Assembly shall, in all cases except treason, felony, or breach of the peace, be privileged from arrest during the sessions of their respective houses; and for any speech or debate in either house shall not be questioned in any other place. They shall not be subject to arrest under any civil process during the sessions of the General Assembly, or during the fifteen days before the beginning or after the ending of any session.

Section 10. Journal of Proceedings

Each house shall keep a journal of its proceedings, which shall be published from time to time. The vote of each member voting in each house on any question shall, at the desire of one-fifth of those present, be recorded in the journal. On the final vote on any bill, and on the vote in any election or impeachment conducted in the General Assembly or on the expulsion of a member, the name of each member voting in each house and how he voted shall be recorded in the journal.

Section 11. Enactment of Laws

No law shall be enacted except by bill. A bill may originate in either house, may be approved or rejected by the other, or may be amended by either, with the concurrence of the other. No bill shall become a law unless, prior to its passage:

(a) it has been referred to a committee of each house, considered by such committee in session, and reported;

(b) it has been printed by the house in which it originated prior to its passage therein;

(c) it has been read by its title, or its title has been printed in a daily calendar, on three different calendar days in each house; and

(d) upon its final passage a vote has been taken thereon in each house, the name of each member voting for and against recorded in the journal, and a majority of those voting in each house, which majority shall include at least two-fifths of the members elected to that house, recorded in the affirmative. Only in the manner required in subparagraph (d) of this section shall an amendment to a bill by one house be concurred in by the other, or a conference report be adopted by either house, or either house discharge a committee from the consideration of a bill and consider the same as if reported. The printing and reading, or either, required in subparagraphs (b) and (c) of this section, may be dispensed with in a bill to codify the laws of the Commonwealth, and in the case of an emergency by a vote of four-fifths of the members voting in each house, the name of each member voting and how he voted to be recorded in the journal.

No bill which creates or establishes a new office, or which creates, continues, or revives a debt or charge, or which makes, continues, or revives any appropriation of public or trust money or property, or which releases, discharges, or commutes any claim or demand of the Commonwealth, or which imposes, continues, or revives a tax, shall be passed except by the affirmative vote of a majority of all the members elected to each house, the name of each member voting and how he voted to be recorded in the journal.

Every law imposing, continuing, or reviving a tax shall specifically state such tax. However, any law by which taxes are imposed may define or specify the subject and provisions of such tax by reference to any provision of the laws of the United States as those laws may be or become effective at any time or from time to time, and may prescribe exceptions or modifications to any such provision.

The presiding officer of each house or upon his inability or failure to act a person designated by a majority of the members elected to each house shall, not later than three days after each bill is enrolled, sign each bill that has been passed by both houses and duly enrolled. The fact of signing shall be recorded in the journal.

Section 12. Form of Laws

No law shall embrace more than one object, which shall be expressed in its title. Nor shall any law be revived or amended with reference to its title, but the act revived or the section amended shall be reenacted and published at length.
Section 13. Effective date of laws.

All laws enacted at a regular session, including laws which are enacted by reason of actions taken during the reconvened session following a regular session, but excluding a general appropriation law, shall take effect on the first day of July following the adjournment of the session of the General Assembly at which it has been enacted; and all laws enacted at a special session, including laws which are enacted by reason of actions taken during the reconvened session following a special session but excluding a general appropriation law, shall take effect on the first day of the fourth month following the month of adjournment of the special session; unless in the case of an emergency (which emergency shall be expressed in the body of the bill) the General Assembly shall specify an earlier date by a vote of four-fifths of the members voting in each house, the name of each member voting and how he voted to be recorded in the journal, or unless a subsequent date is specified in the body of the bill or by general law.

Section 14. Powers of General Assembly; Limitations

The authority of the General Assembly shall extend to all subjects of legislation not herein forbidden or restricted; and a specific grant of authority in this Constitution upon a subject shall not work a restriction of its authority upon the same or any other subject. The omission in this Constitution of specific grants of authority heretofore conferred shall not be construed to deprive the General Assembly of such authority, or to indicate a change of policy in reference thereto, unless such purpose plainly appear.

The General Assembly shall confer on the courts power to grant divorces, change the names of persons, and direct the sales of estates belonging to infants and other persons under legal disabilities, and shall not, by special legislation, grant relief in these or other cases of which the courts or other tribunals may have jurisdiction.

The General Assembly may regulate the exercise by courts of the right to punish for contempt. The General Assembly's power to define the accrual date for a civil action based on an intentional tort committed by a natural person against a person who, at the time of the intentional tort, was a minor shall include the power to provide for the retroactive application of a change in the accrual date. No natural person shall have a constitutionally protected property right to bar a cause of action based on intentional torts as described herein on the ground that a change in the accrual date for the action has been applied retroactively or that a statute of limitations or statute of repose has expired.

The General Assembly shall not enact any local, special, or private law in the following cases:

(1) For the punishment of crime.

(2) Providing a change of venue in civil or criminal cases.

(3) Regulating the practice in, or the jurisdiction of, or changing the rules of evidence in any judicial proceedings or inquiry before the courts or other tribunals, or providing or changing the methods of collecting debts or enforcing judgments or prescribing the effect of judicial sales of real estate.

(4) Changing or locating county seats.

(5) For the assessment and collection of taxes, except as to animals which the General Assembly may deem dangerous to the farming interests.

(6) Extending the time for the assessment or collection of taxes.

(7) Exempting property from taxation.

(8) Remitting, releasing, postponing, or diminishing any obligation or liability of any person, corporation, or association to the Commonwealth or to any political subdivision thereof.

(9) Refunding money lawfully paid into the treasury of the Commonwealth or the treasury of any political subdivision thereof.

(10) Granting from the treasury of the Commonwealth, or granting or authorizing to be granted from the treasury of any political subdivision thereof, any extra compensation to any public officer, servant, agent, or contractor.

(11) For registering voters, conducting elections, or designating the places of voting.

(12) Regulating labor, trade, mining, or manufacturing, or the rate of interest on money.

(13) Granting any pension.

(14) Creating, increasing, or decreasing, or authorizing to be created, increased, or decreased, the salaries, fees, percentages, or allowances of public officers during the term for which they are elected or appointed.

(15) Declaring streams navigable, or authorizing the construction of booms or dams therein, or the removal of obstructions therefrom.

(16) Affecting or regulating fencing or the boundaries of land, or the running at large of stock.

(17) Creating private corporations, or amending, renewing, or extending the charters thereof.

(18) Granting to any private corporation, association, or individual any special or exclusive right, privilege, or immunity.

(19) Naming or changing the name of any private corporation or association.

(20) Remitting the forfeiture of the charter of any private corporation, except upon the condition that such corporation shall thereafter hold its charter subject to the provisions of this Constitution and the laws passed in pursuance thereof.

Section 15. General Laws

In all cases enumerated in the preceding section, and in every other case which, in its judgment, may be provided for by general laws, the General Assembly shall enact general laws. Any general law shall be subject to amendment or repeal, but the amendment or partial repeal thereof shall not operate directly or indirectly to enact, and shall not have the effect of enactment of, a special, private, or local law.

No general or special law shall surrender or suspend the right and power of the Commonwealth, or any political subdivision thereof, to tax corporations and corporate property, except as authorized by Article X. No private corporation, association, or individual shall be specially exempted from the operation of any general law, nor shall a general law's operation be suspended for the benefit of any private corporation, association, or individual.
Section 16. Appropriations to religious or charitable bodies.
The General Assembly shall not make any appropriation of public funds, personal property, or real estate to any church or sectarian society, or any association or institution of any kind whatever which is entirely or partly, directly or indirectly, controlled by any church or sectarian society. Nor shall the General Assembly make any like appropriation to any charitable institution which is not owned or controlled by the Commonwealth; the General Assembly may, however, make appropriations to nonsectarian institutions for the reform of youthful criminals and may also authorize counties, cities, or towns to make such appropriations to any charitable institution or association.

Section 17. Impeachment

The Governor, Lieutenant Governor, Attorney General, judges, members of the State Corporation Commission, and all officers appointed by the Governor or elected by the General Assembly, offending against the Commonwealth by malfeasance in office, corruption, neglect of duty, or other high crime or misdemeanor may be impeached by the House of Delegates and prosecuted before the Senate, which shall have the sole power to try impeachments. When sitting for that purpose, the senators shall be on oath or affirmation, and no person shall be convicted without the concurrence of two-thirds of the senators present. Judgment in case of impeachment shall not extend further than removal from office and disqualification to hold and enjoy any office of honor, trust, or profit under the Commonwealth; but the person convicted shall nevertheless be subject to indictment, trial, judgment, and punishment according to law. The Senate may sit during the recess of the General Assembly for the trial of impeachments.

Section 18. Auditor of Public Accounts

An Auditor of Public Accounts shall be elected by the joint vote of the two houses of the General Assembly for the term of four years. His powers and duties shall be prescribed by law.

ARTICLE V: EXECUTIVE

Section 1. Executive Power; Governor's Term of Office

The chief executive power of the Commonwealth shall be vested in a Governor. He shall hold office for a term commencing upon his inauguration on the Saturday after the second Wednesday in January, next succeeding his election, and ending in the fourth year thereafter immediately upon the inauguration of his successor. He shall be ineligible to the same office for the term next succeeding that for which he was elected, and to any other office during his term of service.

Section 2. Election of Governor

The Governor shall be elected by the qualified voters of the Commonwealth at the time and place of choosing members of the General Assembly. Returns of the election shall be transmitted, under seal, by the proper officers, to the State Board of Elections, or such other officer or agency as may be designated by law, which shall cause the returns to be opened and the votes to be counted in the manner prescribed by law. The person having the highest number of votes shall be declared elected; but if two or more shall have the highest and an equal number of votes, one of them shall be chosen Governor by a majority of the total membership of the General Assembly. Contested elections for Governor shall be decided by a like vote. The mode of proceeding in such cases shall be prescribed by law.

Section 3. Qualifications of Governor

No person except a citizen of the United States shall be eligible to the office of Governor; nor shall any person be eligible to that office unless he shall have attained the age of thirty years and have been a resident of the Commonwealth and a registered voter in the Commonwealth for five years next preceding his election.

Section 4. Place of Residence and Compensation of Governor

The Governor shall reside at the seat of government. He shall receive for his services a compensation to be prescribed by law, which shall neither be increased nor diminished during the period for which he shall have been elected. While in office he shall receive no other emolument from this or any other government.

Section 5. Legislative Responsibilities of Governor

The Governor shall communicate to the General Assembly, at every regular session, the condition of the Commonwealth, recommend to its consideration such measures as he may deem expedient, and convene the General Assembly on application of two-thirds of the members elected to each house thereof, or when, in his opinion, the interest of the Commonwealth may require.

Section 6. Presentation of Bills; Powers of Governor; Vetoes and Amendments

(a) Every bill which passes the Senate and House of Delegates, before it becomes law, shall be presented to the Governor.

(b) During a regular or special session, the Governor shall have seven days in which to act on the bill after it is presented to him and to exercise one of the three options set out below. If the Governor does not act on the bill, it shall become law without his signature.

(i) The Governor may sign the bill if he approves it, and the bill shall become law.

(ii) The Governor may veto the bill if he objects to it by returning the bill with his objections to the house in which the bill originated. The house shall enter the objections in its journal and reconsider the bill. The house may override the veto by a two-thirds vote of the members present, which two-thirds shall include a majority of the members elected to that house. If the house of origin overrides the Governor's veto, it shall send the bill and Governor's objections to the other house where the bill shall be reconsidered. The second house may override the Governor's veto by a two-thirds vote of the members present, which two-thirds shall include a majority of the members elected to that house. If both houses override the Governor's veto, the bill shall become law without his signature. If either house fails to override the Governor's veto, the veto shall stand and the bill shall not become law.

(iii) The Governor may recommend one or more specific and severable amendments to a bill by returning it with his recommendation to the house in which it originated. The house shall enter the Governor's recommendation in its journal and reconsider the bill. If both houses agree to the Governor's entire recommendation, the bill, as amended, shall become law. Each house may agree to the Governor's amendments by a majority vote of the members present. If both houses agree to the bill in the form originally sent to the Governor by a two-thirds vote of all members present in each house, which two-thirds shall include a majority of the members elected to that house, the original bill shall become law. If the Governor sends down specific and severable amendments then each house may determine, in accordance with its own procedures, whether to act on the Governor's amendments en bloc or individually, or any combination thereof. If the house of origin agrees to one or more of the Governor's amendments, it shall send the bill and the entire recommendation to the other house. The second house may also agree to one or more of the Governor's amendments. If either house fails to agree to the Governor's entire recommendation or fails to agree to at least one of the Governor's amendments agreed to by the other house, the bill, as originally presented to the Governor, shall be returned to the Governor. If both houses agree to one or more amendments but not to the entire recommendation of the Governor, the bill shall be re-enrolled with the Governor's amendments agreed to by both houses and shall be returned to the Governor. If the

Governor fails to send down specific and severable amendments as determined by the majority vote of the members present in either house, then the bill shall be before that house, in the form originally sent to the Governor and may be acted upon in accordance with Article IV, Section 11 of this Constitution and returned to the Governor. The Governor shall either sign or veto a bill returned as provided in this subsection or, if there are fewer than seven days remaining in the session, as provided in subsection (c).

(c) When there are fewer than seven days remaining in the regular or special session from the date a bill is presented to the Governor and the General Assembly adjourns to a reconvened session, the Governor shall have thirty days from the date of adjournment of the regular or special session in which to act on the bills presented to him and to exercise one of the three options set out below. If the Governor does not act on any bill, it shall become law without his signature.

(i) The Governor may sign the bill if he approves it, and the bill shall become law.

(ii) The Governor may veto the bill if he objects to it by returning the bill with his objections to the house in which the bill originated. The same procedures for overriding his veto are applicable as stated in subsection (b) for bills vetoed during the session.

(iii) The Governor may recommend one or more specific and severable amendments to a bill by returning it with his recommendation to the house in which it originated. The same procedures for considering his recommendation are applicable as stated in subsection (b) (iii) for bills returned with his recommendation. The Governor shall either sign or veto a bill returned to him from a reconvened session. If the Governor vetoes the bill, the veto shall stand and the bill shall not become law. If the Governor does not act on the bill within thirty days after the adjournment of the reconvened session, the bill shall become law without his signature.

(d) The Governor shall have the power to veto any particular item or items of an appropriation bill, but the veto shall not affect the item or items to which he does not object. The item or items objected to shall not take effect except in the manner provided in this section for a bill vetoed by the Governor.

(e) In all cases set forth above, the names of the members voting for and against the bill, the amendment or amendments to the bill, or the item or items of an appropriation bill shall be entered on the journal of each house.

Section 7. Executive and Administrative Powers

The Governor shall take care that the laws be faithfully executed. The Governor shall be commander-in-chief of the armed forces of the Commonwealth and shall have power to embody such forces to repel invasion, suppress insurrection, and enforce the execution of the laws.

The Governor shall conduct, either in person or in such manner as shall be prescribed by law, all intercourse with other and foreign states.

The Governor shall have power to fill vacancies in all offices of the Commonwealth for the filling of which the Constitution and laws make no other provision. If such office be one filled by the election of the people, the appointee shall hold office until the next general election, and thereafter until his successor qualifies, according to law. The General Assembly shall, if it is in session, fill vacancies in all offices which are filled by election by that body.

Gubernatorial appointments to fill vacancies in offices which are filled by election by the General Assembly or by appointment by the Governor which is subject to confirmation by the Senate or the General Assembly, made during the recess of the General

Assembly, shall expire at the end of thirty days after the commencement of the next session of the General Assembly.

Section 8. Information from Administrative Officers

The Governor may require information in writing, under oath, from any officer of any executive or administrative department, office, or agency, or any public institution upon any subject relating to their respective departments, offices, agencies, or public institutions; and he may inspect at any time their official books, accounts, and vouchers, and ascertain the conditions of the public funds in their charge, and in that connection may employ accountants. He may require the opinion in writing of the Attorney General upon any question of law affecting the official duties of the Governor.

Section 9. Administrative Organization

The functions, powers, and duties of the administrative departments and divisions and of the agencies of the Commonwealth within the legislative and executive branches may be prescribed by law.

Section 10. Appointment and Removal of Administrative Officers

Except as may be otherwise provided in this Constitution, the Governor shall appoint each officer serving as the head of an administrative department or division of the executive branch of the government, subject to such confirmation as the General Assembly may prescribe. Each officer appointed by the Governor pursuant to this section shall have such professional qualifications as may be prescribed by law and shall serve at the pleasure of the Governor.

Section 11. Effect of Refusal of General Assembly to Confirm an Appointment by the Governor

No person appointed to any office by the Governor, whose appointment is subject to confirmation by the General Assembly, under the provisions of this Constitution or any statute, shall enter upon, or continue in, office after the General Assembly shall have refused to confirm his appointment, nor shall such person be eligible for reappointment during the recess of the General Assembly to fill the vacancy caused by such refusal to confirm.

Section 12. Executive Clemency

The Governor shall have power to remit fines and penalties under such rules and regulations as may be prescribed by law; to grant reprieves and pardons after conviction except when the prosecution has been carried on by the House of Delegates; to remove political disabilities consequent upon conviction for offenses committed prior or subsequent to the adoption of this Constitution; and to commute capital punishment.

He shall communicate to the General Assembly, at each regular session, particulars of every case of fine or penalty remitted, of reprieve or pardon granted, and of punishment commuted, with his reasons for remitting, granting, or commuting the same.

Section 13. Lieutenant Governor; Election and Qualifications

A Lieutenant Governor shall be elected at the same time and for the same term as the Governor, and his qualifications and the manner and ascertainment of his election, in all respects, shall be the same, except that there shall be no limit on the terms of the Lieutenant Governor.

Section 14. Duties and Compensation of Lieutenant Governor

The Lieutenant Governor shall be President of the Senate but shall have no vote except in case of an equal division. He shall receive for his services a compensation to be prescribed by law, which shall not be increased nor diminished during the period for which he shall have been elected.

Section 15. Attorney General

An Attorney General shall be elected by the qualified voters of the Commonwealth at the same time and for the same term as the Governor; and the fact of his election shall be ascertained in the same manner. No person shall be eligible for election or appointment to the office of Attorney General unless he is a citizen of the United States, has attained the age of thirty years, and has the qualifications required for a judge of a court of record. He shall perform such duties and receive such compensation as may be prescribed by law, which compensation shall neither be increased nor diminished during the period for which he shall have been elected. There shall be no limit on the terms of the Attorney General.

Section 16. Succession to the Office of Governor

When the Governor-elect is disqualified, resigns, or dies following his election but prior to taking office, the Lieutenant Governor-elect shall succeed to the office of Governor for the full term. When the Governor-elect fails to assume office for any other reason, the Lieutenant Governor-elect shall serve as Acting Governor.

Whenever the Governor transmits to the President pro tempore of the Senate and the Speaker of the House of Delegates his written declaration that he is unable to discharge the powers and duties of his office and until he transmits to them a written declaration to the contrary, such powers and duties shall be discharged by the Lieutenant Governor as Acting Governor.

Whenever the Attorney General, the President pro tempore of the Senate, and the Speaker of the House of Delegates, or a majority of the total membership of the General Assembly, transmit to the Clerk of the Senate and the Clerk of the House of Delegates their written declaration that the Governor is unable to discharge the powers and duties of his office, the Lieutenant Governor shall immediately assume the powers and duties of the office as Acting Governor.

Thereafter, when the Governor transmits to the Clerk of the Senate and the Clerk of the House of Delegates his written declaration that no inability exists, he shall resume the powers and duties of his office unless the Attorney General, the President pro tempore of the Senate, and the Speaker of the House of Delegates, or a majority of the total membership of the General Assembly, transmit within four days to the Clerk of the Senate and the Clerk of the House of Delegates their written declaration that the Governor is unable to discharge the powers and duties of his office. Thereupon the General Assembly shall decide the issue, convening within forty-eight hours for that purpose if not already in session. If within twenty-one days after receipt of the latter declaration or, if the General Assembly is not in session, within twenty-one days after the General Assembly is required to convene, the General Assembly determines by three-fourths vote of the elected membership of each house of the General Assembly that the Governor is unable to discharge the powers and duties of his office, the Lieutenant Governor shall become Governor; otherwise, the Governor shall resume the powers and duties of his office.

In the case of the removal of the Governor from office or in the case of his disqualification, death, or resignation, the Lieutenant Governor shall become Governor.

If a vacancy exists in the office of Lieutenant Governor when the Lieutenant Governor is to succeed to the office of Governor or to serve as Acting Governor, the Attorney General, if he is eligible to serve as Governor, shall succeed to the office of Governor for the unexpired term or serve as Acting Governor. If the Attorney General is ineligible to serve as Governor, the Speaker of the House of Delegates, if he is eligible to serve as Governor, shall succeed to the office of Governor for the unexpired term or serve as Acting Governor. If a vacancy exists in the office of the Speaker of the House of Delegates or if the Speaker of the House of Delegates is ineligible to serve as Governor, the House of Delegates shall convene and fill the vacancy.

In the event of an emergency or enemy attack upon the soil of Virginia and a resulting inability of the House of Delegates to convene to fill the vacancy, the Speaker of the House, the person designated to act in his stead as prescribed in the Rules of the House of Delegates, the President pro tempore of the Senate, or the majority leader of the Senate, in that designated order, shall serve as Acting Governor until such time as the House of Delegates convenes to elect a Governor.

The General Assembly may provide by law for the waiver of the eligibility requirements for the Attorney General, Speaker of the House, or acting Speaker to serve as Governor or Acting Governor in the event of an emergency or enemy attack upon the soil of Virginia as evidenced by a proclamation of the Governor or alternative authority prescribed by law.

Section 17. Commissions and Grants

Commissions and grants shall run in the name of the Commonwealth of Virginia, and be attested by the Governor, with the seal of the Commonwealth annexed.

ARTICLE VI: JUDICIARY

Section 1. Judicial Power; Jurisdiction

The judicial power of the Commonwealth shall be vested in a Supreme Court and in such other courts of original or appellate jurisdiction subordinate to the Supreme Court as the General Assembly may from time to time establish. Trial courts of general jurisdiction, appellate courts, and such other courts as shall be so designated by the General Assembly shall be known as courts of record.

The Supreme Court shall, by virtue of this Constitution, have original jurisdiction in cases of habeas corpus, mandamus, and prohibition; to consider claims of actual innocence presented by convicted felons in such cases and in such manner as may be provided by the General Assembly; in matters of judicial censure, retirement, and removal under Section 10 of this article, and to answer questions of state law certified by a court of the United States or the highest appellate court of any other state. All other jurisdiction of the Supreme Court shall be appellate. Subject to such reasonable rules as may be prescribed as to the course of appeals and other procedural matters, the Supreme Court shall, by virtue of this Constitution, have appellate jurisdiction in cases involving the constitutionality of a law under this Constitution or the Constitution of the United States and in cases involving the life or liberty of any person.

The General Assembly may allow the Commonwealth the right to appeal in all cases, including those involving the life or liberty of a person, provided such appeal would not otherwise violate this Constitution or the Constitution of the United States.

Subject to the foregoing limitations, the General Assembly shall have the power to determine the original and appellate jurisdiction of the courts of the Commonwealth.

Section 2. Supreme Court

The Supreme Court shall consist of seven justices. The General Assembly may, if three-fifths of the elected membership of each house so vote at two successive regular sessions, increase or decrease the number of justices of the Court, provided that the Court shall consist of no fewer than seven and no more than eleven justices. The Court may sit and render final judgment en banc or in divisions as may be prescribed by law. No decision shall become the judgment of the Court, however, except on the concurrence of at least three justices, and no law shall be declared unconstitutional under either this Constitution or the Constitution of the United States except on the concurrence of at least a majority of all justices of the Supreme Court.

Section 3. Selection of Chief Justice

The Chief Justice shall be selected from among the justices in a manner provided by law.

Section 4. Administration of the Judicial System

The Chief Justice of the Supreme Court shall be the administrative head of the judicial system. He may temporarily assign any judge of a court of record to any other court of record except the Supreme Court and may assign a retired judge of a court of record, with his consent, to any court of record except the Supreme Court. The General Assembly may adopt such additional measures as it deems desirable for the improvement of the administration of justice by the courts and for the expedition of judicial business.

Section 5. Rules of Practice and Procedure

The Supreme Court shall have the authority to make rules governing the course of appeals and the practice and procedures to be used in the courts of the Commonwealth, but such rules shall not be in conflict with the general law as the same shall, from time to time, be established by the General Assembly.

Section 6. Opinions and Judgments of the Supreme Court

When a judgment or decree is reversed, modified, or affirmed by the Supreme Court, or when original cases are resolved on their merits, the reasons for the Court's action shall be stated in writing and preserved with the record of the case. The Court may, but need not, remand a case for a new trial. In any civil case, it may enter final judgment, except that the award in a suit or action for unliquidated damages shall not be increased or diminished.

Section 7. Selection and Qualification of Judges

The justices of the Supreme Court shall be chosen by the vote of a majority of the members elected to each house of the General Assembly for terms of twelve years. The judges of all other courts of record shall be chosen by the vote of a majority of the members elected to each house of the General Assembly for terms of eight years. During any vacancy which may exist while the General Assembly is not in session, the Governor may appoint a successor to serve until thirty days after the commencement of the next session of the General Assembly. Upon election by the General Assembly, a new justice or judge shall begin service of a full term.

All justices of the Supreme Court and all judges of other courts of record shall be residents of the Commonwealth and shall, at least five years prior to their appointment or election, have been admitted to the bar of the Commonwealth. Each judge of a trial court of record shall during his term of office reside within the jurisdiction of one of the courts to which he was appointed or elected; provided, however, that where the boundary of such jurisdiction is changed by annexation or otherwise, no judge thereof shall thereby become disqualified from office or ineligible for reelection if, except for such annexation or change, he would otherwise be qualified.

Section 8. Additional Judicial Personnel

The General Assembly may provide for additional judicial personnel, such as judges of courts not of record and magistrates or justices of the peace, and may prescribe their jurisdiction and provide the manner in which they shall be selected and the terms for which they shall serve.

The General Assembly may confer upon the clerks of the several courts having probate jurisdiction, jurisdiction of the probate of wills and of the appointment and qualification of guardians, personal representatives, curators, appraisers, and committees of persons adjudged insane or convicted of felony, and in the matter of the substitution of trustees.

Section 9. Commission; Compensation; Retirement

All justices of the Supreme Court and all judges of other courts of record shall be commissioned by the Governor. They shall receive such salaries and allowances as shall be prescribed by the General Assembly, which shall be apportioned between the Commonwealth and its cities and counties in the manner provided by law. Unless expressly prohibited or limited by the General Assembly, cities and counties shall be permitted to supplement from local funds the salaries of any judges serving within their geographical boundaries. The salary of any justice or judge shall not be diminished during his term of office.

The General Assembly may enact such laws as it deems necessary for the retirement of justices and judges, with such conditions, compensation, and duties as it may prescribe. The General Assembly may also provide for the mandatory retirement of justices and judges after they reach a prescribed age, beyond which they shall not serve, regardless of the term to which elected or appointed.

Section 10. Disabled and Unfit Judges

The General Assembly shall create a Judicial Inquiry and Review Commission consisting of members of the judiciary, the bar, and the public and vested with the power to investigate charges which would be the basis for retirement, censure, or removal of a judge. The Commission shall be authorized to conduct hearings and to subpoena witnesses and documents. Proceedings and documents before the Commission may be confidential as provided by the General Assembly in general law. If the Commission finds the charges to be well-founded, it may file a formal complaint before the Supreme Court.

Upon the filing of a complaint, the Supreme Court shall conduct a hearing in open court and, upon a finding of disability which is or is likely to be permanent and which seriously interferes with the performance by the judge of his duties, shall retire the judge from office. A judge retired under this authority shall be considered for the purpose of retirement benefits to have retired voluntarily.

If the Supreme Court after the hearing on the complaint finds that the judge has engaged in misconduct while in office, or that he has persistently failed to perform the duties of his office, or that he has engaged in conduct prejudicial to the proper administration of justice, it shall censure him or shall remove him from office. A judge removed under this authority shall not be entitled to retirement benefits, but only to the return of contributions made by him, together with any income accrued thereon.

This section shall apply to justices of the Supreme Court, to judges of other courts of record, and to members of the State Corporation Commission. The General Assembly also may provide by general law for the retirement, censure, or removal of judges of any court not of record, or other personnel exercising judicial functions.

Section 11. Incompatible Activities

No justice or judge of a court of record shall, during his continuance in office, engage in the practice of law within or without the Commonwealth, or seek or accept any nonjudicial elective office, or hold any other office of public trust, or engage in any other incompatible activity.

Section 12. Limitation; Judicial Appointment

No judge shall be granted the power to make any appointment of any local governmental official elected by the voters except to fill a vacancy in office pending the next ensuing general election or, if the vacancy occurs within one hundred twenty days prior to such election, pending the second ensuing general election, unless such election falls within sixty days of the end of the term of the office to be filled.

ARTICLE VII: LOCAL GOVERNMENT

Section 1. Definitions

As used in this article

(1) "county" means any existing county or any such unit hereafter created,

(2) "city" means an independent incorporated community which became a city as provided by law before noon on the first day of July, nineteen hundred seventy-one, or which has within defined boundaries a population of 5,000 or more and which has become a city as provided by law,

(3) "town" means any existing town or an incorporated community within one or more counties which became a town before noon, July one, nineteen hundred seventy-one, as provided by law or which has within defined boundaries a population of 1,000 or more and which has become a town as provided by law,

(4) "regional government" means a unit of general government organized as provided by law within defined boundaries, as determined by the General Assembly,

(5) "general law" means a law which on its effective date applies alike to all counties, cities, towns, or regional governments or to a reasonable classification thereof, and

(6) "special act" means a law applicable to a county, city, town, or regional government and for enactment shall require an affirmative vote of two-thirds of the members elected to each house of the General Assembly.

The General Assembly may increase by general law the population minima provided in this article for cities and towns. Any county which on the effective date of this Constitution had adopted an optional form of government pursuant to a valid statute that does not meet the general law requirements of this article may continue its form of government without regard to such general law requirements until it adopts a form of government provided in conformity with this article. In this article, whenever the General Assembly is authorized or required to act by general law, no special act for that purpose shall be valid unless this article so provides.

Section 2. Organization and Government

The General Assembly shall provide by general law for the organization, government, powers, change of boundaries, consolidation, and dissolution of counties, cities, towns, and regional governments. The General Assembly may also provide by general law optional plans of government for counties, cities, or towns to be effective if approved by a majority vote of the qualified voters voting on any such plan in any such county, city, or town.

The General Assembly may also provide by special act for the organization, government, and powers of any county, city, town, or regional government, including such powers of legislation, taxation, and assessment as the General Assembly may determine, but no such special act shall be adopted which provides for the extension or contraction of boundaries of any county, city, or town.

Every law providing for the organization of a regional government shall, in addition to any other requirements imposed by the General Assembly, require the approval of the organization of the regional government by a majority vote of the qualified voters voting thereon in each county and city which is to participate in the regional government and of the voters voting thereon in a part of a county or city where only the part is to participate.

Section 3. Powers

The General Assembly may provide by general law or special act that any county, city, town, or other unit of government may exercise any of its powers or perform any of its functions and may participate in the financing thereof jointly or in cooperation with the Commonwealth or any other unit of government within or without the Commonwealth. The General Assembly may provide by general law or special act for transfer to or sharing with a regional government of any services, functions, and related facilities of any county, city, town, or other unit of government within the boundaries of such regional government.

Section 4. County and City Officers

There shall be elected by the qualified voters of each county and city a treasurer, a sheriff, an attorney for the Commonwealth, a clerk, who shall be clerk of the court in the office of which deeds are recorded, and a commissioner of revenue. The duties and compensation of such officers shall be prescribed by general law or special act.

Regular elections for such officers shall be held on Tuesday after the first Monday in November. Such officers shall take office on the first day of the following January unless otherwise provided by law and shall hold their respective offices for the term of four years, except that the clerk shall hold office for eight years. The General Assembly may provide for county or city officers or methods of their selection, including permission for two or more units of government to share the officers required by this section, without regard to the provisions of this section, either

(1) by general law to become effective in any county or city when submitted to the qualified voters thereof in an election held for such purpose and approved by a majority of those voting thereon in each such county or city, or

(2) by special act upon the request, made after such an election, of each county or city affected. No such law shall reduce the term of any person holding an office at the time the election is held. A county or city not required to have or to elect such officers prior to the effective date of this Constitution shall not be so required by this section.

The General Assembly may provide by general law or special act for additional officers and for the terms of their office.
Section 5. County, city, and town governing bodies.

The governing body of each county, city, or town shall be elected by the qualified voters of such county, city, or town in the manner provided by law.

If the members are elected by district, the district shall be composed of contiguous and compact territory and shall be so constituted as to give, as nearly as is practicable, representation in proportion to the population of the district. When members are so elected by district, the governing body of any county, city, or town may, in a manner provided by law, increase or diminish the number, and change the boundaries, of districts, and shall in 1971 and every ten years thereafter, and also whenever the boundaries of such districts are changed, reapportion the representation in the governing body among the districts in a manner provided by law. Whenever the governing body of any such unit shall fail to perform the duties so prescribed in the manner herein directed, a suit shall lie on behalf of any citizen thereof to compel performance by the governing body.
Unless otherwise provided by law, the governing body of each city or town shall be elected on the second Tuesday in June and take office on the first day of the following September. Unless otherwise provided by law, the governing body of each county shall be elected on the Tuesday after the first Monday in November and take office on the first day of the following January.

Section 6. Multiple Offices

Unless two or more units exercise functions jointly as authorized in Sections 3 and 4, no person shall at the same time hold more than one office mentioned in this article. No member of a governing body shall be eligible, during the term of office for which he was elected or appointed, to hold any office filled by the governing body by election or appointment, except that a member of a governing body may be named a member of such other boards, commissions, and bodies as may be permitted by general law and except that a member of a governing body may be elected or appointed to fill a vacancy in the office of mayor or board chairman if permitted by general law or special act.

Section 7. Procedures

No ordinance or resolution appropriating money exceeding the sum of five hundred dollars, imposing taxes, or authorizing the borrowing of money shall be passed except by a recorded affirmative vote of a majority of all members elected to the governing body. In case of the veto of such an ordinance or resolution, where the power of veto exists, it shall require for passage thereafter a recorded affirmative vote of two-thirds of all members elected to the governing body.

On final vote on any ordinance or resolution, the name of each member voting and how he voted shall be recorded.

Section 8. Consent to use Public Property

No street railway, gas, water, steam or electric heating, electric light or power, cold storage, compressed air, viaduct, conduit, telephone, or bridge company, nor any corporation, association, person, or partnership engaged in these or like enterprises shall be permitted to use the streets, alleys, or public grounds of a city or town without the previous consent of the corporate authorities of such city or town.

Section 9. Sale of Property and Granting of Franchises by Cities and Towns

No rights of a city or town in and to its waterfront, wharf property, public landings, wharves, docks, streets, avenues, parks, bridges, or other public places, or its gas, water, or electric works shall be sold except by an ordinance or resolution passed by a recorded affirmative vote of three-fourths of all members elected to the governing body.

No franchise, lease, or right of any kind to use any such public property or any other public property or easement of any description in a manner not permitted to the general public shall be granted for a longer period than forty years, except for air rights together with easements for columns of support, which may be granted for a period not exceeding sixty years. Before granting any such franchise or privilege for a term in excess of five years, except for a trunk railway, the city or town shall, after due advertisement, publicly receive bids therefor. Such grant, and any contract in pursuance thereof, may provide that upon the termination of the grant, the plant as well as the property, if any, of the grantee in the streets, avenues, and other public places shall thereupon, without compensation to the grantee, or upon the payment of a fair valuation therefor, become the property of the said city or town; but the grantee shall be entitled to no payment by reason of the value of the franchise. Any such plant or property acquired by a city or town may be sold or leased or, unless prohibited by general law, maintained, controlled, and operated by such city or town. Every such grant shall specify the mode of determining any valuation therein provided for and shall make adequate provisions by way of forfeiture of the grant, or otherwise, to secure efficiency of public service at reasonable rates and the maintenance of the property in good order throughout the term of the grant.

Section 10. Debt

(a) No city or town shall issue any bonds or other interest-bearing obligations which, including existing indebtedness, shall at any time exceed ten per centum of the assessed valuation of the real estate in the city or town subject to taxation, as shown by the last preceding assessment for taxes. In determining the limitation for a city or town there shall not be included the following classes of indebtedness:

(1) Certificates of indebtedness, revenue bonds, or other obligations issued in anticipation of the collection of the revenues of such city or town for the then current year; provided that such certificates, bonds, or other obligations mature within one year from the date of their issue, be not past due, and do not exceed the revenue for such year.

(2) Bonds pledging the full faith and credit of such city or town authorized by an ordinance enacted in accordance with Section 7, and approved by the affirmative vote of the qualified voters of the city or town voting upon the question of their issuance, for a supply of water or other specific undertaking from which the city or town may derive a revenue; but from and after a period to be determined by the governing body not exceeding five years from the date of such election, whenever and for so long as such undertaking fails to produce sufficient revenue to pay for cost of operation and administration (including interest on bonds issued therefor), the cost of insurance against loss by injury to persons or property, and an annual amount to be placed into a sinking fund sufficient to pay the bonds at or before maturity, all outstanding bonds issued on account of such undertaking shall be included in determining such limitation.

(3) Bonds of a city or town the principal and interest on which are payable exclusively from the revenues and receipts of a water system or other specific undertaking or undertakings from which the city or town may derive a revenue or secured, solely or together with such revenues, by contributions of other units of government.

(4) Contract obligations of a city or town to provide payments over a period of more than one year to any publicly owned or controlled regional project, if the project has been authorized by an interstate compact or if the General Assembly by general law or special act has authorized an exclusion for such project purposes.

(b) No debt shall be contracted by or on behalf of any county or district thereof or by or on behalf of any regional government or district thereof except by authority conferred by the General Assembly by general law. The General Assembly shall not authorize any such debt, except the classes described in paragraphs (1) and (3) of subsection (a), refunding bonds, and bonds issued, with the consent of the school board and the governing body of the county, by or on behalf of a county or district thereof for capital projects for school purposes and sold to the Literary Fund, the Virginia Supplemental Retirement System, or other State agency prescribed by law, unless in the general law authorizing the same, provision be made for submission to the qualified voters of the county or district thereof or the region or district thereof, as the case may be, for approval or rejection by a majority vote of the qualified voters voting in an election on the question of contracting such debt. Such approval shall be a prerequisite to contracting such debt.

Any county may, upon approval by the affirmative vote of the qualified voters of the county voting in an election on the question, elect to be treated as a city for the purposes of issuing its bonds under this section. If a county so elects, it shall thereafter be subject to all of the benefits and limitations of this section applicable to cities, but in determining the limitation for a county there shall be included, unless otherwise excluded under this section, indebtedness of any town or district in that county empowered to levy taxes on real estate.

ARTICLE VIII: EDUCATION

Section 1. Public Schools of High Quality to be Maintained

The General Assembly shall provide for a system of free public elementary and secondary schools for all children of school age throughout the Commonwealth, and shall seek to ensure that an educational program of high quality is established and continually maintained.

Section 2. Standards of Quality; State and Local Support of Public Schools

Standards of quality for the several school divisions shall be determined and prescribed from time to time by the Board of Education, subject to revision only by the General Assembly. The General Assembly shall determine the manner in which funds are to be provided for the cost of maintaining an educational program meeting the prescribed standards of quality, and shall provide for the apportionment of the cost of such program between the Commonwealth and the local units of government comprising such school divisions. Each unit of local government shall provide its portion of such cost by local taxes or from other available funds.

Section 3. Compulsory Education; Free Textbooks

The General Assembly shall provide for the compulsory elementary and secondary education of every eligible child of appropriate age, such eligibility and age to be determined by law. It shall ensure that textbooks are provided at no cost to each child attending public school whose parent or guardian is financially unable to furnish them.

Section 4. Board of Education

The general supervision of the public school system shall be vested in a Board of Education of nine members, to be appointed by the Governor, subject to confirmation by the General Assembly. Each appointment shall be for four years, except that those to fill vacancies shall be for the unexpired terms. Terms shall be staggered, so that no more than three regular appointments shall be made in the same year.

Section 5. Powers and Duties of the Board of Education

The powers and duties of the Board of Education shall be as follows:

(a) Subject to such criteria and conditions as the General Assembly may prescribe, the Board shall divide the Commonwealth into school divisions of such geographical area and school-age population as will promote the realization of the prescribed standards of quality, and shall periodically review the adequacy of existing school divisions for this purpose.

(b) It shall make annual reports to the Governor and the General Assembly concerning the condition and needs of public education in the Commonwealth, and shall in such report identify any school divisions which have failed to establish and maintain schools meeting the prescribed standards of quality.

(c) It shall certify to the school board of each division a list of qualified persons for the office of division superintendent of schools, one of whom shall be selected to fill the post by the division school board. In the event a division school board fails to select a division superintendent within the time prescribed by law, the Board of Education shall appoint him.

(d) It shall have authority to approve textbooks and instructional aids and materials for use in courses in the public schools of the Commonwealth.

(e) Subject to the ultimate authority of the General Assembly, the Board shall have primary responsibility and authority for effectuating the educational policy set forth in this article, and it shall have such other powers and duties as may be prescribed by law.

Section 6. Superintendent of Public Instruction

A Superintendent of Public Instruction, who shall be an experienced educator, shall be appointed by the Governor, subject to confirmation by the General Assembly, for a term coincident with that of the Governor making the appointment, but the General Assembly may alter by statute this method of selection and term of office. The powers and duties of the Superintendent shall be prescribed by law.

Section 7. School Boards

The supervision of schools in each school division shall be vested in a school board, to be composed of members selected in the manner, for the term, possessing the qualifications, and to the number provided by law.

Section 8. The Literary Fund

The General Assembly shall set apart as a permanent and perpetual school fund the present Literary Fund; the proceeds of all public lands donated by Congress for free public school purposes, of all escheated property, of all waste and unappropriated lands, of all property accruing to the Commonwealth by forfeiture except as hereinafter provided, of all fines collected for offenses committed against the Commonwealth, and of the annual interest on the Literary Fund; and such other sums as the General Assembly may appropriate. But so long as the principal of the Fund totals as much as eighty million dollars, the General Assembly may set aside all or any part of additional moneys received into its principal for public school purposes, including the teachers retirement fund.

The General Assembly may provide by general law an exemption from this section for the proceeds from the sale of all property seized and forfeited to the Commonwealth for a violation of the criminal laws of this Commonwealth proscribing the manufacture, sale or distribution of a controlled substance or marijuana. Such proceeds shall be paid into the state treasury and shall be distributed by law for the purpose of promoting law enforcement. The Literary Fund shall be held and administered by the Board of Education in such manner as may be provided by law. The General Assembly may authorize the Board to borrow other funds against assets of the Literary Fund as collateral, such borrowing not to involve the full faith and credit of the Commonwealth.

The principal of the Fund shall include assets of the Fund in other funds or authorities which are repayable to the Fund.

Section 9. Other Educational Institutions

The General Assembly may provide for the establishment, maintenance, and operation of any educational institutions which are desirable for the intellectual, cultural, and occupational development of the people of this Commonwealth. The governance of such institutions, and the status and powers of their boards of visitors or other governing bodies, shall be as provided by law.

Section 10. State Appropriations Prohibited to Schools or Institutions of Learning not Owned or Exclusively Controlled by The State or Some Subdivision Thereof; Exceptions to Rule

No appropriation of public funds shall be made to any school or institution of learning not owned or exclusively controlled by the State or some political subdivision thereof; provided, first, that the General Assembly may, and the governing bodies of the several counties, cities and towns may, subject to such limitations as may be imposed by the General Assembly, appropriate funds for educational purposes which may be expended in furtherance of elementary, secondary, collegiate or graduate education of Virginia students in public and nonsectarian private schools and institutions of learning, in addition to those owned or exclusively controlled by the State or any such county, city or town; second, that the General Assembly may appropriate funds to an agency, or to a school or institution of learning owned or controlled by an agency, created and established by two or more States under a joint agreement to which this State is a party for the purpose of providing educational facilities for the citizens of the several States joining in such agreement; third, that counties, cities, towns, and districts may make appropriations to nonsectarian schools of manual, industrial, or technical training, and also to any school or institution of learning owned or exclusively controlled by such county, city, town, or school district.

Section 11. Aid to Non-public Higher Education

The General Assembly may provide for loans to, and grants to or on behalf of, students attending nonprofit institutions of higher education in the Commonwealth whose primary purpose is to provide collegiate or graduate education and not to provide religious training or theological education. The General Assembly may also provide for a State agency or authority to assist in borrowing money for construction of educational facilities at such institutions, provided that the Commonwealth shall not be liable for any debt created by such borrowing. The General Assembly may also provide for the Commonwealth or any political subdivision thereof to contract with such institutions for the provision of educational or other related services.

ARTICLE IX: CORPORATIONS

Section 1. State Corporation Commission

There shall be a permanent commission which shall be known as the State Corporation Commission and which shall consist of three members. The General Assembly may, by majority vote of the members elected to each house, increase the size of the Commission to no more than five members. Members of the Commission shall be elected by the General Assembly and shall serve for regular terms of six years. At least one member of the Commission shall have the qualifications prescribed for judges of courts of record, and any Commissioner may be impeached or removed in the manner provided for the impeachment or removal of judges of courts of record. The General Assembly may enact such laws as it deems necessary for the retirement of the Commissioners, with such conditions, compensation, and duties as it may prescribe. The General Assembly may also provide for the mandatory retirement of Commissioners after they reach a prescribed age, beyond which they shall not serve, regardless of the term to which elected or appointed. Whenever a vacancy in the Commission shall occur or exist when the General Assembly is in session, the General Assembly shall elect a successor for such unexpired term. If the General Assembly is not in session, the Governor shall forthwith appoint pro tempore a qualified person to fill the vacancy for a term ending thirty days after the commencement of the next regular session of the General Assembly and the General Assembly shall elect a successor for such unexpired term.

The Commission shall annually elect one of its members chairman. Its subordinates and employees, and the manner of their appointment and removal, shall be as provided by law, except that its heads of divisions and assistant heads of divisions shall be appointed and subject to removal by the Commission.

Section 2. Powers and Duties of the Commission

Subject to the provisions of this Constitution and to such requirements as may be prescribed by law, the Commission shall be the department of government through which shall be issued all charters, and amendments or extensions thereof, of domestic corporations and all licenses of foreign corporations to do business in this Commonwealth.

Except as may be otherwise prescribed by this Constitution or by law, the Commission shall be charged with the duty of administering the laws made in pursuance of this Constitution for the regulation and control of corporations doing business in this Commonwealth. Subject to such criteria and other requirements as may be prescribed by law, the Commission shall have the power and be charged with the duty of regulating the rates, charges, and services and, except as may be otherwise authorized by this Constitution or by general law, the facilities of railroad, telephone, gas, and electric companies.

The Commission shall in proceedings before it ensure that the interests of the consumers of the Commonwealth are represented, unless the General Assembly otherwise provides for representation of such interests.

The Commission shall have such other powers and duties not inconsistent with this Constitution as may be prescribed by law.

Section 3. Procedures of the Commission

Before promulgating any general order, rule, or regulation, the Commission shall give reasonable notice of its contents.
In all matters within the jurisdiction of the Commission, it shall have the powers of a court of record to administer oaths, to compel the attendance of witnesses and the production of documents, to punish for contempt, and to enforce compliance with its lawful orders or requirements by adjudging and enforcing by its own appropriate process such fines or other penalties as

may be prescribed or authorized by law. Before the Commission shall enter any finding, order, or judgment against a party it shall afford such party reasonable notice of the time and place at which he shall be afforded an opportunity to introduce evidence and be heard.

The Commission may prescribe its own rules of practice and procedure not inconsistent with those made by the General Assembly. The General Assembly shall have the power to adopt such rules, to amend, modify, or set aside the Commission's rules, or to substitute rules of its own.

Section 4. Appeals from Actions of the Commission

The Commonwealth, any party in interest, or any party aggrieved by any final finding, order, or judgment of the Commission shall have, of right, an appeal to the Supreme Court. The method of taking and prosecuting an appeal from any action of the Commission shall be prescribed by law or by the rules of the Supreme Court. All appeals from the Commission shall be to the Supreme Court only.

No other court of the Commonwealth shall have jurisdiction to review, reverse, correct, or annul any action of the Commission or to enjoin or restrain it in the performance of its official duties, provided, however, that the writs of mandamus and prohibition shall lie from the Supreme Court to the Commission.
Section 5. Foreign corporations.

No foreign corporation shall be authorized to carry on in this Commonwealth the business of, or to exercise any of the powers or functions of, a public service enterprise, or be permitted to do anything which domestic corporations are prohibited from doing, or be relieved from compliance with any of the requirements made of similar domestic corporations by the Constitution and laws of this Commonwealth. However, nothing in this section shall restrict the power of the General Assembly to enact such laws specially applying to foreign corporations as the General

Assembly may deem appropriate.

Section 6. Corporations Subject to General Laws

The creation of corporations, and the extension and amendment of charters whether heretofore or hereafter granted, shall be provided for by general law, and no charter shall be granted, amended, or extended by special act, nor shall authority in such matters be conferred upon any tribunal or officer, except to ascertain whether the applicants have, by complying with the requirements of the law, entitled themselves to the charter, amendment, or extension applied for and to issue or refuse the same accordingly. Such general laws may be amended, repealed, or modified by the General Assembly. Every corporation chartered in this Commonwealth shall be deemed to hold its charter and all amendments thereof under the provisions of, and subject to all the requirements, terms, and conditions of, this Constitution and any laws passed in pursuance thereof. The police power of the Commonwealth to regulate the affairs of corporations, the same as individuals, shall never be abridged.

Section 7. Exclusions from Term "Corporation" or "Company"

The term "corporation" or "company" as used in this article shall exclude all municipal corporations, other political subdivisions, and public institutions owned or controlled by the Commonwealth.

ARTICLE X. TAXATION AND FINANCE

Section 1. Taxable Property; Uniformity; Classification and Segregation

All property, except as hereinafter provided, shall be taxed. All taxes shall be levied and collected under general laws and shall be uniform upon the same class of subjects within the territorial limits of the authority levying the tax, except that the General Assembly may provide for differences in the rate of taxation to be imposed upon real estate by a city or town within all or parts of areas added to its territorial limits, or by a new unit of general government, within its area, created by or encompassing two or more, or parts of two or more, existing units of general government. Such differences in the rate of taxation shall bear a reasonable relationship to differences between non-revenue producing governmental services giving land urban character which are furnished in one or several areas in contrast to the services furnished in other areas of such unit of government. The General Assembly may by general law and within such restrictions and upon such conditions as may be prescribed authorize the governing body of any county, city, town or regional government to provide for differences in the rate of taxation imposed upon tangible personal property owned by persons not less than sixty-five years of age or persons permanently and totally disabled as established by general law who are deemed by the General Assembly to be bearing an extraordinary tax burden on said tangible personal property in relation to their income and financial worth.

The General Assembly may define and classify taxable subjects. Except as to classes of property herein expressly segregated for either State or local taxation, the General Assembly may segregate the several classes of property so as to specify and determine upon what subjects State taxes, and upon what subjects local taxes, may be levied.

Section 2. Assessments

All assessments of real estate and tangible personal property shall be at their fair market value, to be ascertained as prescribed by law. The General Assembly may define and classify real estate devoted to agricultural, horticultural, forest, or open space uses, and may by general law authorize any county, city, town, or regional government to allow deferral of, or relief from, portions of taxes otherwise payable on such real estate if it were not so classified, provided the General Assembly shall first determine that classification of such real estate for such purpose is in the public interest for the preservation or conservation of real estate for such uses. In the event the General Assembly defines and classifies real estate for such purposes, it shall prescribe the limits, conditions, and extent of such deferral or relief. No such deferral or relief shall be granted within the territorial limits of any county, city, town, or regional government except by ordinance adopted by the governing body thereof. So long as the Commonwealth shall levy upon any public service corporation a State franchise, license, or other similar tax based upon or measured by its gross receipts or gross earnings, or any part thereof, its real estate and tangible personal property shall be assessed by a central State agency, as prescribed by law.
Section 3. Taxes or assessments upon abutting property owners. The General Assembly by general law may authorize any county, city, town, or regional government to impose taxes or assessments upon abutting property owners for such local public improvements as may be designated by the General Assembly; however, such taxes or assessments shall not be in excess of the peculiar benefits resulting from the improvements to such abutting property owners.

Section 4. Property Segregated for Local Taxation; Exceptions

Real estate, coal and other mineral lands, and tangible personal property, except the rolling stock of public service corporations, are hereby segregated for, and made subject to, local taxation only, and shall be assessed for local taxation in such manner and at such times as the General Assembly may prescribe by general law.

Section 5. Franchise Taxes; Taxation of Corporate Stock

The General Assembly, in imposing a franchise tax upon corporations, may in its discretion make the same in lieu of taxes upon other property, in whole or in part, of such corporations. Whenever a franchise tax shall be imposed upon a corporation doing business in this Commonwealth, or whenever all the capital, however invested, of a corporation chartered under the laws of this Commonwealth shall be taxed, the shares of stock issued by any such corporation shall not be further taxed.
Section 6. Exempt property.

(a) Except as otherwise provided in this Constitution, the following property and no other shall be exempt from taxation, State and local, including inheritance taxes:

(1) Property owned directly or indirectly by the Commonwealth or any political subdivision thereof, and obligations of the Commonwealth or any political subdivision thereof exempt by law.

(2) Real estate and personal property owned and exclusively occupied or used by churches or religious bodies for religious worship or for the residences of their ministers.

(3) Private or public burying grounds or cemeteries, provided the same are not operated for profit.

(4) Property owned by public libraries or by institutions of learning not conducted for profit, so long as such property is primarily used for literary, scientific, or educational purposes or purposes incidental thereto. This provision may also apply to leasehold interests in such property as may be provided by general law.

(5) Intangible personal property, or any class or classes thereof, as may be exempted in whole or in part by general law.

(6) Property used by its owner for religious, charitable, patriotic, historical, benevolent, cultural, or public park and playground purposes, as may be provided by classification or designation by an ordinance adopted by the local governing body and subject to such restrictions and conditions as provided by general law.

(7) Land subject to a perpetual easement permitting inundation by water as may be exempted in whole or in part by general law.

(b) The General Assembly may by general law authorize the governing body of any county, city, town, or regional government to provide for the exemption from local property taxation, or a portion thereof, within such restrictions and upon such conditions as may be prescribed, of real estate and personal property designed for continuous habitation owned by, and occupied as the sole dwelling of, persons not less than sixty-five years of age or persons permanently and totally disabled as established by general law. A local governing body may be authorized to establish either income or financial worth limitations, or both, in order to qualify for such relief.

(c) Except as to property of the Commonwealth, the General Assembly by general law may restrict or condition, in whole or in part, but not extend, any or all of the above exemptions.

(d) The General Assembly may define as a separate subject of taxation any property, including real or personal property, equipment, facilities, or devices, used primarily for the purpose of abating or preventing pollution of the atmosphere or waters of the Commonwealth or for the purpose of transferring or storing solar energy, and by general law may allow the governing body of any county, city, town, or regional government to exempt or partially exempt such property from taxation, or by general law may directly exempt or partially exempt such property from taxation.

(e) The General Assembly may define as a separate subject of taxation household goods, personal effects and tangible farm property and products, and by general law may allow the governing body of any county, city, town, or regional government to exempt or partially exempt such property from taxation, or by general law may directly exempt or partially exempt such property from taxation.

(f) Exemptions of property from taxation as established or authorized hereby shall be strictly construed; provided, however, that all property exempt from taxation on the effective date of this section shall continue to be exempt until otherwise provided by the General Assembly as herein set forth.

(g) The General Assembly may by general law authorize any county, city, town, or regional government to impose a service charge upon the owners of a class or classes of exempt property for services provided by such governments.

(h) The General Assembly may by general law authorize the governing body of any county, city, town, or regional government to provide for a partial exemption from local real property taxation, within such restrictions and upon such conditions as may be prescribed, (i) of real estate whose improvements, by virtue of age and use, have undergone substantial renovation, rehabilitation or replacement or (ii) of real estate with new structures and improvements in conservation, redevelopment, or rehabilitation areas.

(i) The General Assembly may by general law allow the governing body of any county, city, or town to exempt or partially exempt from taxation any generating equipment installed after December thirty-one, nineteen hundred seventy-four, for the purpose of converting from oil or natural gas to coal or to wood, wood bark, wood residue, or to any other alternate energy source for manufacturing, and any co-generation equipment installed since such date for use in manufacturing.

(j) The General Assembly may by general law allow the governing body of any county, city, or town to have the option to exempt or partially exempt from taxation any business, occupational or professional license or any merchants' capital, or both.

Section 6-A. Property Tax Exemption for Certain Veterans and Surviving Spouses of Soldiers Killed in Action

(a) Notwithstanding the provisions of Section 6, the General Assembly by general law, and within the restrictions and conditions prescribed therein, shall exempt from taxation the real property, including the joint real property of husband and wife, of any veteran who has been determined by the United States Department of Veterans Affairs or its successor agency pursuant to federal law to have a one hundred percent service-connected, permanent, and total disability, and who occupies the real property as his or her principal place of residence. The General Assembly shall also provide this exemption from taxation for real property owned by the surviving spouse of a veteran who was eligible for the exemption provided in this subdivision, so long as the surviving spouse does not remarry and continues to occupy the real property as his or her principal place of residence.

(b) Notwithstanding the provisions of Section 6, the General Assembly by general law, and within the restrictions and conditions prescribed therein, may exempt from taxation the real property of the surviving spouse of any member of the armed forces of the United States who was killed in action as determined by the United States Department of Defense, who occupies the real property as his or her principal place of residence. The exemption under this subdivision shall cease if the surviving spouse remarries and shall not be claimed thereafter. This exemption applies regardless of whether the spouse was killed in action prior to the effective date of this subdivision, but the exemption shall not be applicable for any period of time prior to the effective date. This exemption applies to the surviving spouse's principal place of residence without any restriction on the spouse's moving to a different principal place of residence and without any requirement that the spouse reside in the Commonwealth at the time of death of the member of the armed forces.

Section 7. Collection and Disposition of State Revenues

All taxes, licenses, and other revenues of the Commonwealth shall be collected by its proper officers and paid into the State treasury. No money shall be paid out of the State treasury except in pursuance of appropriations made by law; and no such appropriation shall be made which is payable more than two years and six months after the end of the session of the General Assembly at which the law is enacted authorizing the same. Other than as may be provided for in the debt provisions of this Constitution, the Governor, subject to such criteria as may be established by the General Assembly, shall ensure that no expenses of the Commonwealth be incurred which exceed total revenues on hand and anticipated during a period not to exceed the two years and six months period established by this section of the Constitution.

Section 7-A. Lottery Proceeds Fund; Distribution of Lottery Revenues

The General Assembly shall establish the Lottery Proceeds Fund. The Fund shall consist of the net revenues of any lottery conducted by the Commonwealth. Lottery proceeds shall be appropriated from the Fund to the Commonwealth's counties, cities and towns, and the school divisions thereof, to be expended for the purposes of public education.

Any county, city, or town which accepts a distribution from the Fund shall provide its portion of the cost of maintaining an educational program meeting the standards of quality prescribed pursuant to Section 2 of Article VIII of this Constitution without the use of distributions from the Fund.

The General Assembly shall enact such laws as may be necessary to implement the Fund and the provisions of this section.

The General Assembly may appropriate amounts from the Fund for other purposes only by a vote of four-fifths of the members voting in each house, the name of each member voting and how he voted to be recorded in the journal of the house.

Section 8. Limit of Tax or Revenue; Revenue Stabilization Fund

No other or greater amount of tax or revenues shall, at any time, be levied than may be required for the necessary expenses of the government, or to pay the indebtedness of the Commonwealth.

The General Assembly shall establish the Revenue Stabilization Fund. The Fund shall consist of an amount not to exceed fifteen percent of the Commonwealth's average annual tax revenues derived from taxes on income and retail sales as certified by the Auditor of Public Accounts for the three fiscal years immediately preceding. The Auditor of Public Accounts shall compute the fifteen percent limitation of such fund annually and report to the General Assembly not later than the first day of December. "Certified tax revenues" means the Commonwealth's annual tax revenues derived from taxes on income and retail sales as certified by the Auditor of Public Accounts.

The General Assembly shall make deposits to the Fund to equal at least fifty percent of the product of the certified tax revenues collected in the most recently ended fiscal year times the difference between the annual percentage increase in the certified tax revenues collected for the most recently ended fiscal year and the average annual percentage increase in the certified tax revenues collected in the six fiscal years immediately preceding the most recently ended fiscal year. However, growth in certified tax revenues, which is the result of either increases in tax rates on income or retail sales or the repeal of exemptions therefrom, may be excluded, in whole or in part, from the computation immediately preceding for a period of time not to exceed six calendar years from the calendar year in which such tax rate increase or exemption repeal was effective. Additional appropriations may be made at any time so long as the fifteen percent limitation established herein is not exceeded. All interest earned on the Fund shall be part thereof; however, if the Fund's balance exceeds the limitation, the amount in excess of the limitation shall be paid into the general fund after appropriation by the General Assembly.

The General Assembly may appropriate an amount for transfer from the Fund to compensate for no more than one-half of the difference between the total general fund revenues appropriated and a revised general fund revenue forecast presented to the General Assembly prior to or during a subsequent regular or special legislative session. However, no transfer shall be made unless the general fund revenues appropriated exceed such revised general fund revenue forecast by more than two percent of certified tax revenues collected in the most recently ended fiscal year. Furthermore, no appropriation or transfer from such fund in any fiscal year shall exceed more than one-half of the balance of the Revenue Stabilization Fund. The General Assembly may enact such laws as may be necessary and appropriate to implement the Fund.

Section 9. State Debt

No debt shall be contracted by or in behalf of the Commonwealth except as provided herein.

(a) Debts to meet emergencies and redeem previous debt obligations.
The General Assembly may

(1) contract debts to suppress insurrection, repel invasion, or defend the Commonwealth in time of war;

(2) contract debts, or may authorize the Governor to contract debts, to meet casual deficits in the revenue or in anticipation of the collection of revenues of the Commonwealth for the then current fiscal year within the amount of authorized appropriations, provided that the total of such indebtedness shall not exceed thirty per centum of an amount equal to 1.15 times the average annual tax revenues of the Commonwealth derived from taxes on income and retail sales, as certified by the Auditor of Public Accounts, for the preceding fiscal year and that each such debt shall mature within twelve months from the date such debt is incurred; and

(3) contract debts to redeem a previous debt obligation of the Commonwealth.

The full faith and credit of the Commonwealth shall be pledged to any debt created under this subsection. The amount of such debt shall not be included in the limitations on debt hereinafter established, except that the amount of debt incurred pursuant to clause (3) above shall be included in determining the limitation on the aggregate amount of general obligation debt for capital projects permitted elsewhere in this article unless the debt so incurred pursuant to clause (3) above is secured by a pledge of net revenues from capital projects of institutions or agencies administered solely by the executive department of the Commonwealth or of institutions of higher learning of the Commonwealth, which net revenues the Governor shall certify are anticipated to be sufficient to pay the principal of and interest on such debt and to provide such reserves as the law authorizing the same may require, in which event the amount thereof shall be included in determining the limitation on the aggregate amount of debt contained in the provision of this article which authorizes general obligation debt for certain revenue-producing capital projects.

(b) General obligation debt for capital projects and sinking fund. The General Assembly may, upon the affirmative vote of a majority of the members elected to each house, authorize the creation of debt to which the full faith and credit of the Commonwealth is pledged, for capital projects to be distinctly specified in the law authorizing the same; provided that any such law shall specify capital projects constituting a single purpose and shall not take effect until it shall have been submitted to the people at an election and a majority of those voting on the question shall have approved such debt. No such debt shall be authorized by the General Assembly if the amount thereof when added to amounts approved by the people or authorized by the General Assembly and not yet submitted to the people for approval, under this subsection during the three fiscal years immediately preceding the authorization by the General Assembly of such debt and the fiscal year in which such debt is authorized shall exceed twenty-five per centum of an amount equal to 1.15 times the average annual tax revenues of the Commonwealth derived from taxes on income and retail sales, as certified by the Auditor of Public Accounts, for the three fiscal years immediately preceding the authorization of such debt by the General Assembly.

No debt shall be incurred under this subsection if the amount thereof when added to the aggregate amount of all outstanding debt to which the full faith and credit of the Commonwealth is pledged other than that excluded from this limitation by the provisions of this article authorizing the contracting of debts to redeem a previous debt obligation of the Commonwealth and for certain revenue-producing capital projects, less any amounts set aside in sinking funds for the repayment of such outstanding debt, shall exceed an amount equal to 1.15 times the average annual tax revenues of the Commonwealth derived from taxes on income and retail sales, as certified by the Auditor of Public Accounts, for the three fiscal years immediately preceding the incurring of such debt.

All debt incurred under this subsection shall mature within a period not to exceed the estimated useful life of the projects as stated in the authorizing law, which statement shall be conclusive, or a period of thirty years, whichever is shorter; and all debt incurred to redeem a previous debt obligation of the Commonwealth, except that which is secured by net revenues anticipated to be sufficient to pay the same and provide reserves therefor, shall mature within a period not to exceed thirty years. Such debt shall be amortized, by payment into a sinking fund or otherwise, in annual installments of principal to begin not later than one-tenth of the term of the bonds, and any such sinking fund shall not be appropriated for any other purpose; if such debt be for public road purposes, such payment shall be first made from revenues segregated by law for the construction and maintenance of State highways. No such installment shall exceed the smallest previous installment by more than one hundred per centum. If sufficient funds are not appropriated in the budget for any fiscal year for the timely payment of the interest upon and installments of principal of such debt, there shall be set apart by direction of the Governor, from the first general fund revenues received during such fiscal year and thereafter, a sum sufficient to pay such interest and installments of principal.

(c) Debt for certain revenue-producing capital projects.
The General Assembly may authorize the creation of debt secured by a pledge of net revenues derived from rates, fees, or other charges and the full faith and credit of the Commonwealth, and such debt shall not be included in determining the limitation on general obligation debt for capital projects as permitted elsewhere in this article, provided that

(1) the creation of such debt is authorized by the affirmative vote of two-thirds of the members elected to each house of the General Assembly; and

(2) such debt is created for specific revenue-producing capital projects (including the enlargement or improvement thereof), which shall be distinctly specified in the law authorizing the same, of institutions and agencies administered solely by the executive department of the Commonwealth or of institutions of higher learning of the Commonwealth.

Before any such debt shall be authorized by the General Assembly, and again before it shall be incurred, the Governor shall certify in writing, filed with the Auditor of Public Accounts, his opinion, based upon responsible engineering and economic estimates, that the anticipated net revenues to be pledged to the payment of principal of and interest on such debt will be sufficient to meet such payments as the same become due and to provide such reserves as the law authorizing such debt may require, and that the projects otherwise comply with the requirements of this subsection, which certifications shall be conclusive.

No debt shall be incurred under this subsection if the amount thereof when added to the aggregate amount of all outstanding debt authorized by this subsection and the amount of all outstanding debt incurred to redeem a previous debt obligation of the Commonwealth which is to be included in the limitation of this subsection by virtue of the provisions of this article authorizing the contracting of debts to redeem a previous debt obligation of the Commonwealth, less any amounts set aside in sinking funds for the payment of such debt, shall exceed an amount equal to 1.15 times the average annual tax revenues of the Commonwealth derived from taxes on income and retail sales, as certified by the Auditor of Public Accounts, for the three fiscal years immediately preceding the incurring of such debt. This subsection shall not be construed to pledge the full faith and credit of the Commonwealth to the payment of any obligation of the Commonwealth, or any institution, agency, or authority thereof, or to any refinancing or re-issuance of such obligation which was incurred prior to the effective date of this subsection.

(d) Obligations to which section not applicable. The restrictions of this section shall not apply to any obligation incurred by the Commonwealth or any institution, agency, or authority thereof if the full faith and credit of the Commonwealth is not pledged or committed to the payment of such obligation.

Section 10. Lending of Credit, Stock Subscriptions, and Works of Internal Improvement

Neither the credit of the Commonwealth nor of any county, city, town, or regional government shall be directly or indirectly, under any device or pretense whatsoever, granted to or in aid of any person, association, or corporation; nor shall the Commonwealth or any such unit of government subscribe to or become interested in the stock or obligations of any company, association, or corporation for the purpose of aiding in the construction or maintenance of its work; nor shall the Commonwealth become a party to or become interested in any work of internal improvement, except public roads and public parks, or engage in carrying on any such work; nor shall the Commonwealth assume any indebtedness of any county, city, town, or regional government, nor lend its credit to the same. This section shall not be construed to prohibit the General Assembly from establishing an authority with power to insure and guarantee loans to finance industrial development and industrial expansion and from making appropriations to such authority.

Section 11. Governmental Employees Retirement System

The General Assembly shall maintain a retirement system for state employees and employees of participating political subdivisions and school divisions. The funds of the retirement system shall be deemed separate and independent trust funds, shall be segregated from all other funds of the Commonwealth, and shall be invested and administered solely in the interests of the members and beneficiaries thereof. Neither the General Assembly nor any public officer, employee, or agency shall use or authorize the use of such trust funds for any purpose other than as provided in law for benefits, refunds, and administrative expenses, including but not limited to legislative oversight of the retirement system. Such trust funds shall be invested as authorized by law. Retirement system benefits shall be funded using methods which are consistent with generally accepted actuarial principles. The retirement system shall be subject to restrictions, terms, and conditions as may be prescribed by the General Assembly.

Section 6-B. Property Tax Exemptions for Spouses of Certain Emergency Services Providers

Notwithstanding the provisions of Section 6, the General Assembly by general law, and within the restrictions and conditions prescribed therein, may provide for a local option to exempt from taxation the real property of the surviving spouse of any law-enforcement officer, firefighter, search and rescue personnel, or emergency medical services personnel who was killed in the line of duty, who occupies the real property as his or her principal place of residence. The exemption under this section shall cease if the surviving spouse remarries and shall not be claimed thereafter. This exemption applies regardless of whether the spouse was killed in the line of duty prior to the effective date of this section, but the exemption shall not be applicable for any period of time prior to the effective date. This exemption applies to the surviving spouse's principal place of residence without any restriction on the spouse's moving to a different principal place of residence and without any requirement that the spouse reside in the Commonwealth at the time of death of the law-enforcement officer, firefighter, search and rescue personnel, or emergency medical services personnel.

ARTICLE XI: CONSERVATION

Section 1. Natural Resources and Historical Sites of the Commonwealth

To the end that the people have clean air, pure water, and the use and enjoyment for recreation of adequate public lands, waters, and other natural resources, it shall be the policy of the Commonwealth to conserve, develop, and utilize its natural resources, its public lands, and its historical sites and buildings. Further, it shall be the Commonwealth's policy to protect its atmosphere, lands, and waters from pollution, impairment, or destruction, for the benefit, enjoyment, and general welfare of the people of the Commonwealth.

Section 2. Conservation and Development of Natural Resources and Historical Sites

In the furtherance of such policy, the General Assembly may undertake the conservation, development, or utilization of lands or natural resources of the Commonwealth, the acquisition and protection of historical sites and buildings, and the protection of its atmosphere, lands, and waters from pollution, impairment, or destruction, by agencies of the Commonwealth or by the creation of public authorities, or by leases or other contracts with agencies of the United States, with other states, with units of government in the Commonwealth, or with private persons or corporations. Notwithstanding the time limitations of the provisions of Article X, Section 7, of this Constitution, the Commonwealth may participate for any period of years in the cost of projects which shall be the subject of a joint undertaking between the Commonwealth and any agency of the United States or of other states.

Section 3. Natural Oyster Beds

The natural oyster beds, rocks, and shoals in the waters of the Commonwealth shall not be leased, rented, or sold but shall be held in trust for the benefit of the people of the Commonwealth, subject to such regulations and restriction as the General Assembly may prescribe, but the General Assembly may, from time to time, define and determine such natural beds, rocks, or shoals by surveys or otherwise.

Section 4. Right of the People to Hunt, Fish, and Harvest Game

The people have a right to hunt, fish, and harvest game, subject to such regulations and restrictions as the General Assembly may prescribe by general law.

ARTICLE XII: FUTURE CHANGES

Section 1. Amendments

Any amendment or amendments to this Constitution may be proposed in the Senate or House of Delegates, and if the same shall be agreed to by a majority of the members elected to each of the two houses, such proposed amendment or amendments shall be entered on their journals, the name of each member and how he voted to be recorded, and referred to the General Assembly at its first regular session held after the next general election of members of the House of Delegates. If at such regular session or any subsequent special session of that General Assembly the proposed amendment or amendments shall be agreed to by a majority of all the members elected to each house, then it shall be the duty of the General Assembly to submit such proposed amendment or amendments to the voters qualified to vote in elections by the people, in such manner as it shall prescribe and not sooner than ninety days after final passage by the General Assembly. If a majority of those voting vote in favor of any amendment, it shall become part of the Constitution on the date prescribed by the General Assembly in submitting the amendment to the voters.

Section 2. Constitutional Convention

The General Assembly may, by a vote of two-thirds of the members elected to each house, call a convention to propose a general revision of, or specific amendments to, this Constitution, as the General Assembly in its call may stipulate.

The General Assembly shall provide by law for the election of delegates to such a convention, and shall also provide for the submission, in such manner as it shall prescribe and not sooner than ninety days after final adjournment of the convention, of the proposals of the convention to the voters qualified to vote in elections by the people. If a majority of those voting vote in favor of any proposal, it shall become effective on the date prescribed by the General Assembly in providing for the submission of the convention proposals to the voters.

Schedule

Section 1. Effective Date of Revised Constitution

This revised Constitution shall, except as is otherwise provided herein, go into effect at noon on the first day of July, nineteen hundred and seventy-one.

Section 2. Officers and Elections

Unless otherwise provided herein or by law, nothing in this revised Constitution shall affect the oath, tenure, term, status, or compensation of any person holding any public office, position, or employment in the Commonwealth, nor affect the date of filling any State or local office, elective or appointive, which shall be filled on the date on which it would otherwise have been filled.

Section 3. Laws, Proceedings, and Obligations Unaffected

The common and statute law in force at the time this revised Constitution goes into effect, so far as not in conflict therewith, shall remain in force until they expire by their own limitation or are altered or repealed by the General Assembly. Unless otherwise provided herein or by law, the adoption of this revised Constitution shall have no effect on pending judicial proceedings or judgments, on any obligations owing to or by the Commonwealth or any of its officers, agencies, or political subdivisions, or on any private obligations or rights.

Section 4. Qualifications of Judges

The requirement of Article VI, Section 7, that justices of the Supreme Court and judges of courts of record shall, at least five years prior to their election or appointment, have been members of the bar of the Commonwealth, shall not preclude justices or judges who were elected or appointed prior to the effective date of this revised Constitution, and who are otherwise qualified,

from completing the term for which they were elected or appointed and from being reelected for one additional term.
Section 5. First session of General Assembly following adoption of revised Constitution.

The General Assembly shall convene at the Capitol at noon on the first Wednesday in January, nineteen hundred and seventy-one. It shall enact such laws as may be deemed proper, including those necessary to implement this revised Constitution. The General Assembly shall reapportion the Commonwealth into electoral districts in accordance with Article II, Section 6, of this Constitution. The General Assembly shall be vested with all the powers, charged with all the duties, and subject to all the limitations prescribed by this Constitution except that this session shall continue as long as may be necessary; that the salary and allowances of members shall not be limited by Section 46 of the Constitution of 1902 as amended and that effective date limitation of Section 53 of the Constitution of 1902 as amended shall not be operative.